First Crochet

First Crochet

Lesley Stanfield

Martingale® & COMPANY

Copyright © Collins & Brown Limited 2005
Text copyright © Lesley Stanfield 2005
Illustrations copyright © Collins & Brown Limited 2005

An imprint of **Chrysalis** Books Group plc
Photographs copyright © Collins & Brown Limited 2005

The rights of Lesley Stanfield to be identified as the author of this work has been
asserted by her in accordance with the Copyright, Designs and Patents Act, 1988.

Edited and designed by Collins & Brown Limited
EDITOR: Jane Ellis
DESIGNER: Penny Stock
PHOTOGRAPHER: Lucinda Symonds & Nicki Dowey
PATTERN CHECKER: Susan Horan

Reproduction by Classic Scan Pte Limited, Singapore
Printed and bound by Kyodo Printing Co Pte Limited, Singapore

Martingale®
& C O M P A N Y

Martingale & Company
20205 144th Avenue NE
Woodinville, WA 98072-8478 USA
www.martingale-pub.com

10 09 08 07 06 05   8 7 6 5 4 3 2 1

ISBN 1-56477-620-4

Mission Statement
Dedicated to providing quality products and service to inspire creativity.

Contents

How to use this book **6**

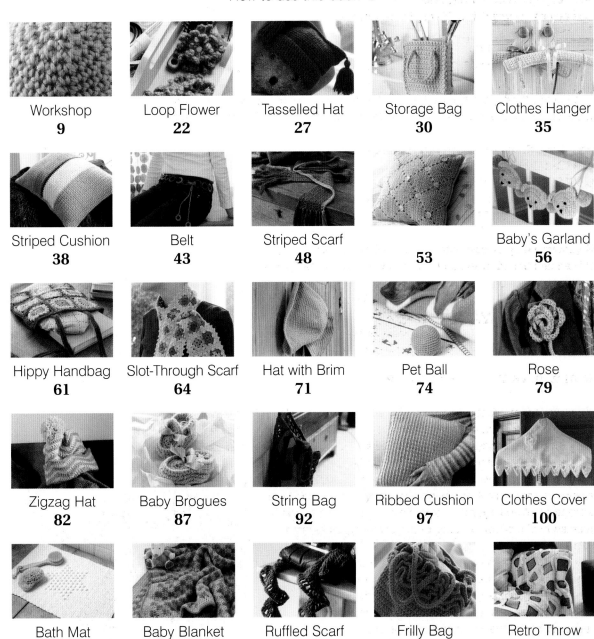

How to use this book

If you have ever watched someone crochet and been fascinated by the darting movement of the hook and the speed with which the work grows you may want to try it for yourself. I know it's a cliché, but it's much easier than it looks! You only have to learn a few simple techniques to be able to make some of the smaller items in this collection. All are designed with the beginner in mind and at the same time to be desirable gifts for yourself or others.

Don't be put off if your first attempts are mis-sized or misshapen. Just experiment with yarn and hook sizes until you feel relaxed and can make the right sort of fabric naturally and easily. It's a great feeling to be a crochet diva!

This book is divided into four chapters: Chain, Slip Stitch and Single Crochet; Double Crochet; Shaping; and Special Effects. The twenty-four projects are graded from very, very easy through to those which require a few more skills. They are all explained with instructions that follow the usual conventions, although abbreviations have been kept to a minimum. These row-by-row and round-by-round instructions are supplemented with pictures of the work in progress. The workshop illustrates the basics. If any additional help is needed the end flaps provide an instant reminder.

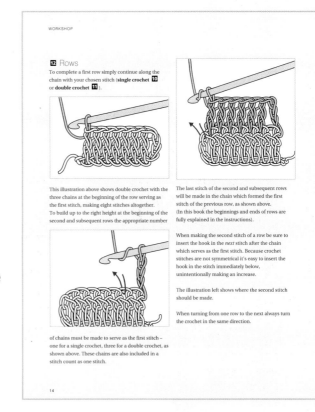

WORKSHOP

12 Rows

To complete a first row simply continue along the chain with your chosen stitch (**single crochet** **10** or **double crochet** **11**).

This illustration above shows double crochet with the three chains at the beginning of the row serving as the first stitch, making eight stitches altogether. To build up to the right height at the beginning of the second and subsequent rows the appropriate number

of chains must be made to serve as the first stitch – one for a single crochet, three for a double crochet, as shown above. These chains are also included in a stitch count as one stitch.

The last stitch of the second and subsequent rows will be made in the chain which formed the first stitch of the previous row, as shown above. (In this book the beginnings and ends of rows are fully explained in the instructions).

When making the second stitch of a row be sure to insert the hook in the *next* stitch after the chain which serves as the first stitch. Because crochet stitches are not symmetrical it's easy to insert the hook in the stitch immediately below, unintentionally making an increase.

The illustration left shows where the second stitch should be made.

When turning from one row to the next always turn the crochet in the same direction.

14

A comprehensive workshop section at the beginning of the book features both diagrams and photographs, so you can see exactly what to do. Easy-to-follow text will teach you all the techniques you need to create the projects in the book. Each technique has a reference number, which is used for cross-referencing in the patterns and on the flaps.

🔟 Gauge

Gauge is the number of stitches and rows to a given measurement. It's essential that your crochet matches the gauge given if the finished size is to be correct. Size isn't critical with many of the projects in this book but it's still a good idea to check your gauge before you begin.

Make a gauge swatch about an inch larger in each direction than the gauge measurement. Insert pins to mark the number of stitches (and rows) given in the tension and then measure the distance between th

...sample above shows how two
...ochet form one ridge – you need to
...when counting rows.

pins (see above). If the measurement doesn't match that in the instructions a larger or smaller hook should be used to achieve the correct result.

🔟 Rounds

Working in rounds means the crochet is all worked on the right side and isn't turned over, so a 'round' can even be square.

There are two methods of working rounds:

1 After a **chain ring** 🔟 has been made, chains make the first stitch of the first round, then stitches are made into the ring and the last stitch is joined to

...sample above shows the slightly
...mation of
...emphasize

The project section features 24 stylish items, starting with the very easiest and moving on to those requiring slightly more skill. Each one is accompanied by clear text and step-by-step photographs showing the key stages, for easy reference as you work. The instructions for each project contain reference numbers which direct you to the relevant technique in the Workshop, should you need to learn a new technique or be reminded of a familiar one.

MAKING THE CUSHION

Square

(make 18)

Chain 🔟 5, **slip stitch** 🔟 into first ch to form a **ring** 🔟.

Working in **rounds** 🔟 with right side facing:

ROUND 1 Ch 3, 2 **double crochet** 🔟 in ring, ch 3, * 3 dc in ring, ch 3;

rep from * twice, sl st to top ch of 3 ch.

ROUND 2 Ch 3,

1 dc in each of next 2 dc, (2 dc, ch 3, 2 dc) in ch sp, * 1 dc in each of next 3 dc, (2 dc, ch 3, 2 dc) in ch sp; rep from * twice, sl st to top ch of 3 ch.

ROUND 3 Ch 3, 1 dc in each of next 4 dc, (2 dc, ch 3,

2 dc) in ch sp, * 1 dc in each of next 7 dc, (2 dc, ch 3, 2 dc) in ch sp; rep from * twice, 1 dc in each of next 2 dc, sl st to top ch of 3 ch.

ROUND 4 Ch 3, 1 dc in each of next 6 dc, (2 dc, ch 3, 2 dc) in ch sp, * 1 dc in each of next 11 dc, (2 dc, ch 3, 2 dc) in ch sp; rep from * twice, 1 dc in each of next 4 dc, sl st to top ch of 3 ch.

Fasten off 🔟.

Finishing

Set out two blocks of 9 squares each, the joins of each round facing in the same direction.

With right sides together, take 2 squares and **join with single crochet** 🔟: insert the hook under 2 strands of the first dc of 15 dc of front square and

under 2 strands of the corresponding dc of the back square, yarn over hook, and pull through a loop, yarn over hook again and pull it through 2 loops to make a sc.

Joining only the groups of 15 dc, join the remaining 7 squares of the back in the same way, then join the 9 squares of the front.

Edging

Back: with right side facing, **join the yarn** 🔟 at one corner and work

(ch 3, 1 dc, ch 3, 2 dc) in corner sp, * 1 dc in each of next 15 dc, (2 dc in last sp of this motif, 1 ch, 2 dc in

first sp of next motif, 1 dc in each of next 15 dc) twice, (2 dc, ch 3, 2 dc) in corner sp; rep from * along each side, joining last side to first with sl st in top ch of 3 ch.

Edge the front to match.

Press to shape.

Take the back and front and join with sc: wrong sides together and working through 2 strands of each pair of stitches, work (ch 1, 2 sc) in one corner sp, * 1 sc in each of next 19 dc, 1 sc in 1-ch sp; rep from * once. 1 sc in each of next 19 dc, 3 sc in corner sp. Continue in this way along 2 more sides, working 3 sc in corners, to the last side and work into the front only along this side to leave an opening for the cushion pad, sl st to 1 ch.

Fasten off.

Sew a button to the center of each square of the front.

Insert the cushion pad and stitch the opening closed.

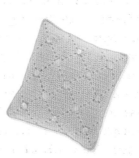

Workshop

Use this section of the book to learn the basics. Handling the yarn and hook will seem awkward at first but repetition will make the movements effortless and you'll quickly gain confidence and speed. Make a slip knot over and over again until you can almost do it with your eyes shut. Then practice the movement which takes the hook under the yarn from left to right, catching the yarn with the end of the hook and pulling it through the loop on the hook. When you have mastered this action you have all the expertise you need. Take the steps one at a time and don't go on to the next until you have really understood the structure of a stitch. Once you have graduated to double crochet you should be able to tackle almost anything.

Getting started

Very few materials are necessary and you probably already have some items, such as a tape measure and small scissors. A blunt-pointed tapestry needle is essential if you are not to split the yarn when sewing pieces together.

Crochet hooks are of different weights as well as sizes, depending on the materials they're made from. It's a good idea to have a selection of sizes so that you can choose the hook that gives you the right gauge and fabric with the yarn you are using.

Choice of yarn is a most important factor and using the yarn specified for the project will eliminate some uncertainty. Otherwise, choose good quality, smooth but not slippery yarn, preferably in a natural fiber. Above all, be prepared to experiment.

1 Holding the hook

For most flexibility hold the hook like a pencil, then you can use your wrist as well as your fingers to manipulate it. You'll need to rotate it slightly, as well as push and pull. Holding the flattened portion gives the right balance. If the pencil grip isn't comfortable, try holding the hook overhand like a knife.

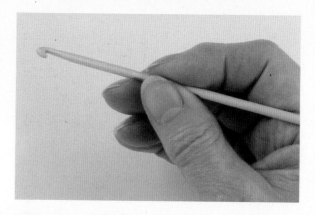

2 Holding the yarn

In the opposite hand the yarn should be threaded through your fingers so that it can be controlled evenly. This hand will also be holding the work as it progresses. There are several ways to hold the yarn. My method is to simply take it over my first three fingers and under my little finger. Many people prefer to put more 'brake' on the yarn by taking it around the little finger. Some thread it under and over other fingers, but all hold the second finger slightly aloft.

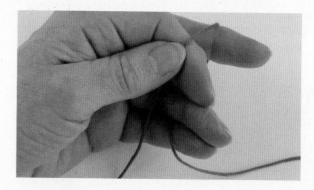

This is essential to hold the yarn fairly taut, ready for hooking. You will have found the best method for you when the yarn is moving easily through your fingers.

3 Making a slip knot

You must first attach the yarn to the hook with a slip knot. There are several ways you can do this but my preferred method is this:

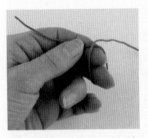 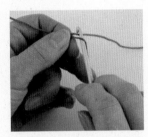

1 Loop the yarn around two fingers.

2 Insert the hook in the loop and catch the long (working) end of the yarn.

3 Pull the yarn through the loop.

4 Hold both ends of the yarn and pull on the hook to tighten the knot.

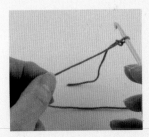

5 Pull on the working end of the yarn to close the knot up to the hook.

4 Yarn over hook

This is the action used in all crochet stitches. The term implies wrapping the yarn around the hook, but in fact the yarn is held taut and the hook manipulated under and over the yarn to catch and then pull it.

Holding the slip knot between thumb and index finger, with the yarn threaded between your fingers as shown in **holding the yarn 2**, flex your hook hand so that the shaft of the hook goes *under* the yarn from front to back – or left to right – and then *over* it to catch the yarn in the hook. Pull the hooked yarn through the loop already on the hook and you will have made a chain. Repeat this action to make a length of chain. This is explained in detail on the following page.

5 Stitches

You now have the basic skills to make any crochet stitch. Chain, slip stitch, single crochet and double crochet are explained in the following pages of the Workshop section. Combinations of these stitches for special effects are explained in the instructions for the projects. All stitches start and finish with a loop on the hook.

6 Chain

Chain is a loop or series of loops which can be used as the foundation of a piece of crochet, as the first stitch of a row or as part of a stitch pattern.

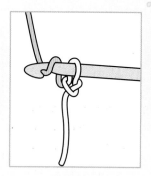

Having made a **slip knot** **3**, take the **yarn over the hook** **4**, then gently pull the yarn through the loop on the hook without tightening it too much. This makes one chain.

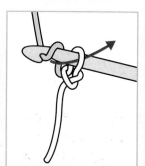 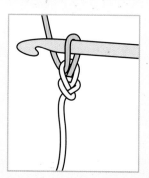

Repeating these actions makes a length of chain. The front of the chain is a series of V shapes (see below left), whereas the formation of the back is more difficult to distinguish. It's always the front that is worked into and the hook inserted under the top two of the three strands that make up a chain.

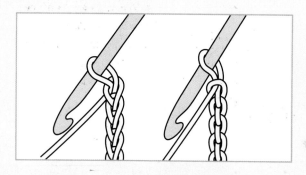

7 Slip stitch

Because it's simply a loop pulled through, in the same way as chain, a slip stitch has no height. It's usually used to join chain into a ring or as an invisible join in a stitch pattern.

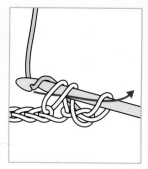

Insert the hook in the chain or stitch, taking it under the two top strands of the chain or stitch. Take the yarn over the hook (see left) and pull it through both the chain or stitch and the loop on the hook. One slip stitch has been made.

8 Making stitches

Always insert the hook in the top two strands of a chain or stitch unless the instructions in the pattern state otherwise.

9 Chain ring

To join a length of chain into a ring with a slip stitch, insert the hook in the first chain, yarn over hook then

pull the yarn through both the chain and the loop on the hook.
A chain ring makes a base for crochet worked in rounds, with the stitches made into the space in the center, not into the chain itself.

10 Single crochet

This is a short stitch which makes a solid fabric when used alone and is a component of many stitch patterns.

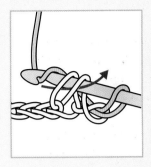

1 When working into a chain, skip one chain (unless instructed otherwise), insert the hook in the next chain, yarn over hook, pull the yarn through the chain to make two loops on the hook.

2 Yarn over hook and pull the yarn through both loops on the hook.

This completes a single crochet, which is the second stitch of the row, the first being the skipped chain.

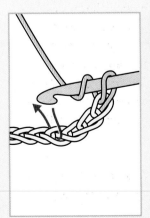

11 Double crochet

This is a taller stitch which is even more versatile for patterning than single crochet.

1 When working into a chain, yarn over hook, skip three chains, insert the hook in the next chain.

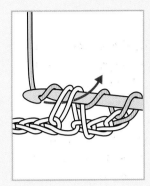

2 Yarn over hook and pull the yarn through the chain to make three loops on the hook.

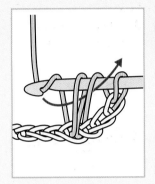

3 Yarn over hook and pull the yarn through the first two loops on the hook.

4 Yarn over hook and pull the yarn through the remaining two loops on the hook.

This completes a double crochet, which is the second stitch of the row, the first being the three skipped chains.

12 Rows

To complete a first row simply continue along the chain with your chosen stitch (**single crochet 10** or **double crochet 11**).

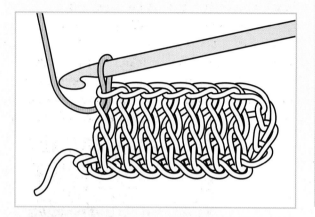

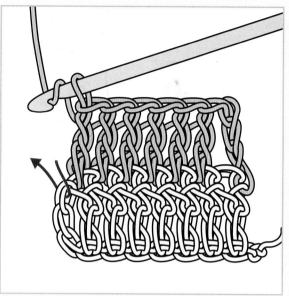

This illustration above shows double crochet with the three chains at the beginning of the row serving as the first stitch, making eight stitches altogether.
To build up to the right height at the beginning of the second and subsequent rows the appropriate number

The last stitch of the second and subsequent rows will be made in the chain which formed the first stitch of the previous row, as shown above.
(In this book the beginnings and ends of rows are fully explained in the instructions).

When making the second stitch of a row be sure to insert the hook in the *next* stitch after the chain which serves as the first stitch. Because crochet stitches are not symmetrical it's easy to insert the hook in the stitch immediately below, unintentionally making an increase.

The illustration at left shows where the second stitch should be made.

When turning from one row to the next always turn the crochet in the same direction.

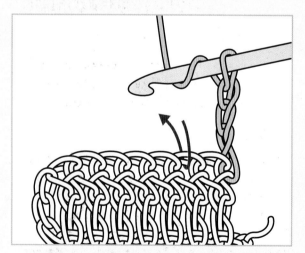

of chains must be made to serve as the first stitch – one for a single crochet, three for a double crochet, as shown above. These chains are also included in a stitch count as one stitch.

The single crochet sample above shows how two rows of single crochet form one ridge – you need to be aware of this when counting rows.

The double crochet sample above shows the slightly asymmetrical formation of crochet stitches, emphasized by being worked in rows.

13 Gauge

Gauge is the number of stitches and rows to a given measurement. It's essential that your crochet matches the gauge given if the finished size is to be correct. Size isn't critical with many of the projects in this book but it's still a good idea to check your gauge before you begin.

Make a gauge swatch about an inch larger in each direction than the gauge measurement. Insert pins to mark the number of stitches (and rows) given in the gauge and then measure the distance between the

pins (see above). If the measurement doesn't match that in the instructions a larger or smaller hook should be used to achieve the correct result.

14 Rounds

Working in rounds means the crochet is all worked on the right side and isn't turned over, so a 'round' can even be square.

There are two methods of working rounds:

1 After a **chain ring** **9** has been made, chains make the first stitch of the first round, then stitches are made into the ring and the last stitch is joined to the chain with a slip stitch. In the same way, subsequent rounds are started with chains and

finished with a slip stitch (see the double crochet sample above).

2 If there's no slip stitch at the end of the first round and no chains starting the next, the rounds will be

continuous with no sign of a join (as shown in the single crochet sample above) but there will be a 'step' at the end.

With continuous rounds, a marker will be needed to keep count of stitches and rounds.

15 Markers

The simplest way to mark rounds is to use a length of contrast yarn. Leaving the ends hanging, lay it from front to back or vice versa between the last

stitch of one round and the first stitch of the next. It will look like a running stitch (see above). On completion, pull it out and discard it.

16 Slip ring

An alternative way to start crochet in the round is with a slip ring. This pulls up tight in the center but is perhaps a little trickier than a chain ring for a beginner. Here it's shown as the basis of a round of double crochet.

1 Make a loop as for a **slip knot 3**.

2 Insert the hook in the loop and catch the working end of the yarn, as for a slip knot.

3 Holding the ring closed with finger and thumb, chain three.

4 Inserting the hook under the two strands formed by the ring and the short end, make the required number of double crochets.

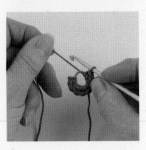

5 Pull on the short end of the yarn to close the ring up before joining with a slip stitch to the top chain of the three chains.

17 Increasing

Increasing can be done at either the beginning or the end of a row. The principle is the same for both single crochet and double crochet.

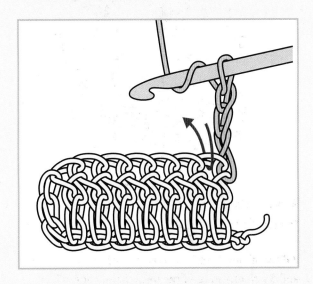

The first diagram above shows where the new stitch is made at the beginning of a row of double crochet.

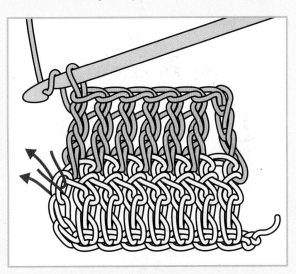

The second diagram shows where two stitches are made at the end of the row.

18 Decreasing

Decreasing a stitch is a little trickier as two stitches must be gathered together. This is done by working half a stitch into each of two adjacent stitches and then completing them as one.

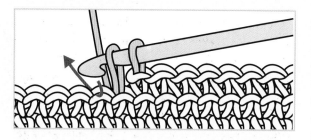

For example, to decrease one stitch in single crochet: * insert the hook in the next stitch, yarn over hook, pull the yarn through;

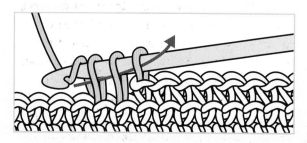

repeat from *, making three loops on the hook, yarn over hook, pull the yarn through all three loops.

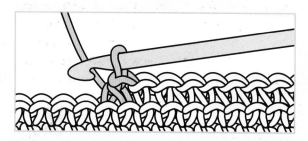

A double-crochet decrease is worked on the same principle, but with the additional wraps and loops of that stitch.

19 Reading instructions

The language of crochet looks mystifying at first, but this is mainly because abbreviations are used. Shortening the instructions makes it easier for you to find your place. You'll quickly learn that ch is chain, sc is single crochet, and you'll have no difficulty following instructions.

Asterisks and brackets are there to help.

An asterisk (*) is simply a marker indicating a point from which a group of instructions is to be repeated. Square brackets also indicate a repeat – in this case, the number of repeats is stated after the brackets. Round brackets indicate a group of stitches to be worked together.

20 Joining new yarn

This is usually done at the beginning or end of a row but it can thicken a seam, so if the crochet is fairly close-textured it can be done mid-stitch and mid-row. Simply leave a short end of the first yarn then, leaving a short end of the new yarn, carry on. After a stitch or two you will be able to pull the two ends to close up any gap and then join them with a reef knot. After completion, undo the knot if it's bulky or leave it if it's not obtrusive, and 'darn in' the ends.

To join new yarn in a new place, for example when starting an edging, hold the yarn behind the work, insert the hook and pull a loop through, yarn over hook and pull it through the loop on the hook.

21 Fastening off

The loop of the last stitch is secured by breaking the yarn and using the hook to gently pull the end

through until the loop is lost. Leave a long end if it will be needed for sewing up.

22 Joining with single crochet

'Sewing up' with a hook instead of a needle is one of the most satisfying aspects of crochet. It's speedy and gives an immaculate finish.

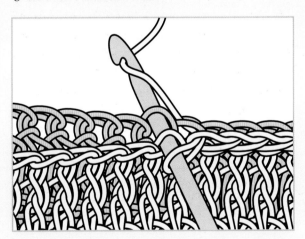

Hold the two pieces of crochet right sides together, insert the hook under the inside single strand of the first stitch of each edge, take the yarn over the hook and pull through a loop, yarn over hook and pull it through both loops on the hook to make a **single**

crochet 10. Continue working single crochet in pairs of stitches in this way (see below left). If a firmer join is required the same method can be used, but inserting the hook under *both* strands of each stitch.

23 Finishing

Most of these projects will need light pressing to make sure they are the correct size and shape, and to give a smooth finish. Lay the item out right side down on a clean padded surface, such as an ironing board, and pin out to shape, with pins at every 2.5cm (1in) all around the edge. For pinning out or holding edges together use long quilting pins which won't get lost in the crochet. Make sure lines of stitches are straight and measure each piece to check it is the correct size. You can stretch or ease a piece to adjust it slightly. Press on the wrong side with a warm iron, using steam if it's advised on the yarn ball band. Before joining motifs, square up squares and pin everything out to size and shape as described above. If you are working with lots of motifs of the same size, a good way of making sure they are identical is to draw a template with a waterproof pen on a piece of plain fabric, and pin them out using this as a guide. Steam or press each motif with a damp cloth according to the instructions on the ball band, then leave to dry before joining together. Large and open pieces of crochet may droop, but if you crochet seams together using the same yarn used for the project, as described in **joining with single crochet 22**, the seams will give in proportion to the rest of the work. Lastly, darn in any ends.

24 Darn in ends

To darn in use a tapestry needle to weave each end invisibly into nearby stitches. End with a back stitch and snip off the end close to the crochet.

1

Chain, slip stitch, and single crochet

The six designs in this section require only the most minimal skills, so if you are a beginner you will need to practice first, but you should soon be able to make something. If you're unhappy with the way the project is turning out just unravel and start again. This sounds like brutal advice but it's better not to persevere hoping that a mistake will correct itself and then be disappointed. That way, you're learning and you're in control!

Loop Flower

Make mop-head flowers for yourself or your friends. They can be used as decoration on a coat, a scarf, or as a hair scrunch.

Chain is usually a base for other stitches, but these flowers are made entirely with chain and slip stitches. A chain ring is filled with chain loops, then chain bars behind are filled with more chain loops.

Size
Approximately 2¼in (6cm) across

You will need
1 x 50g ball of Jaeger Matchmaker Merino Aran in pink
5.50mm (Size I/9 U.S.) hook

Abbreviations
Ch – chain; sl st – slip stitch

MAKING THE FLOWER

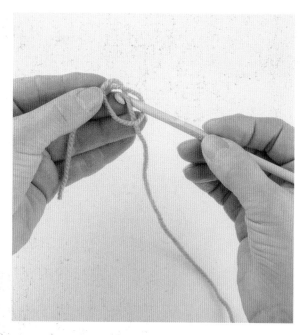

Make a **slip knot 3** .

Chain **6** 4.

Slip stitch 7 into the first ch to form a **chain ring 9** .

ROUND 1 [Ch 10, sl st into ring] 8 times. 8 loops.

ROUND 2 [ch 3, take ch behind 2 loops and sl st into ring] 4 times. This creates 4 bars behind the loops.

tip On round 1 work the slip stitches around the tail end of the yarn as well as the chain of the ring and you will then have one less end to darn in.

ROUND 3 *Working behind loops, into next bar sl st, [ch 10, sl st] 4 times; repeat from * 3 times. 4 loops worked in each bar.

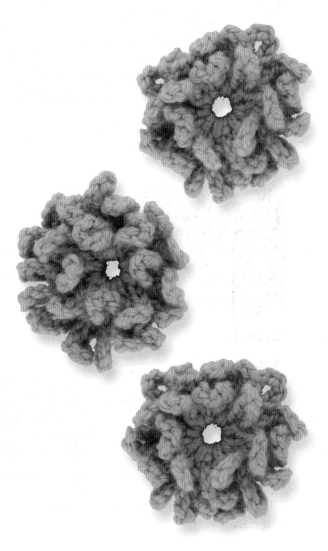

Fasten off 21.
Darn in ends 24.

Tasselled Hat

Swinging tassels are a fun addition to this simplest of all hats.

The hat is a continuous tube of single crochet which, instead of being stitched at the top, is joined with a row of single crochet. Simply add tassels.

Size
To fit age 3–6 months

You will need
2 x 50g balls of Debbie Bliss Merino DK in orange
4.50mm (Size 7 U.S.) hook

Gauge
17 stitches and 20 rounds to 4in (10cm) over sc

Abbreviations
Ch – chain; cm – centimeters; in – inches; sc – single crochet

MAKING THE HAT

Chain  64. Without twisting ch,

slip stitch [7] into first ch to **form a ring** [9].
63 stitches.

ROUND 1 Work 1 **single crochet** [10] in each ch.

With the right side facing,

continue to work in **rounds** [14] of sc for 7½ in
(19cm).
Fasten off [21] but do not break yarn.
JOINING ROW **Join with single crochet** [22]. With the
right side still facing, yarn to the right and

holding the top edge closed: ch 1, *insert hook under
both strands of next sc of front and corresponding

sc of back, yarn over hook and pull a loop through, yarn over hook again and pull it through 2 loops to make a sc in the usual way; repeat from * to end. Fasten off .

Darn in ends 24 .

Finishing

Fold back the brim.

Use another strand of yarn to bind the tassel just below the top. Knot the doubled yarn at the head of the tassel and use this to stitch a tassel to each corner of the hat.

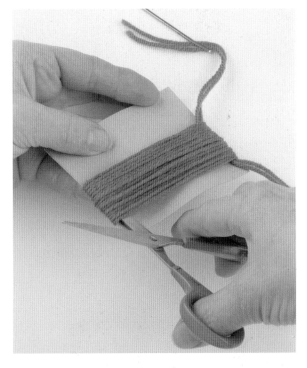

Tassels

Wind yarn around a 3½in (9cm) wide piece of card, enclosing a doubled strand at the top. Cut the yarn along the opposite edge.

Storage Bag

A miniature tote bag makes a practical present in itself or it could be the container for a small gift.

Rows of single crochet make the rectangles which form the sides and base of the bag, while the handles are slip stitch worked into chain.

Size
4½in (11cm) high, 4in (10cm) wide, 2½in (7cm) deep

You will need
1 x 100g ball of Sirdar Pure Cotton DK in turquoise
3.50mm (Size E/4 U.S.) hook
Tapestry needle

Gauge
8 sts and 10 rows to 2in (5cm) over sc

Abbreviations
Cm – centimeters; ch – chain; in – inches;
rep – repeat; sc – single crochet; sts – stitches

MAKING THE BAG

Base

The bag is worked back and forth in **rows** 🔢 .
Chain 6️⃣ 17.

ROW 1 Skip 2 ch, * 1 **single crochet** 🔟 in next ch; rep
from * to end. 16 sts. Turn.
ROW 2 Ch 1, [1 sc in next sc] 14 times,

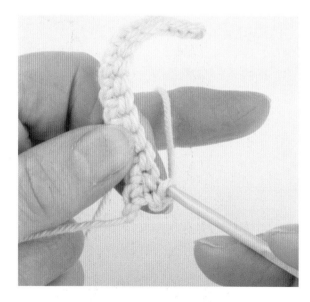

1 sc in top ch of 2 ch. Turn.
ROW 3 Ch 1, [1 sc in next sc] 14 times, 1 sc in ch. Turn.
** Rep last row 9 times. Total 12 rows.
Fasten off 2️⃣1️⃣ .

Back

Work as for base to **.
Rep last row 19 times. Total 22 rows.
Fasten off.

Front

Work as for back.

Sides

(make 2)
Ch 12.
ROW 1 Skip 2 ch, * 1 sc in next ch; rep from * to end.
11 sts. Turn.
ROW 2 Ch 1, [1 sc in next sc] 9 times, 1 sc in top ch of
2 ch. Turn.
ROW 3 Ch 1, [1 dc in next dc] 9 times, 1 dc in ch.
Rep last row 19 times. Total 22 rows.
Fasten off.

Handles

(make 2)
Ch 48.

Skip 1 ch, ***slip stitch** 7️⃣ in next ch; rep from *
to end.
Fasten off.
Darn in ends 2️⃣4️⃣ .

Finishing

With wrong sides together and stitches lying in the same direction,

use a tapestry needle to join a side to the back with stab stitch and an occasional back stitch, taking the needle under two strands of each stitch each time. Join the second side to the back in the same way and then join the sides to the front. With wrong sides together, join the base in the same way.

Use the crochet hook to pull the end of one handle from outside to inside between stitches on the back, then do the same with the other end. Knot both ends. Attach the second handle to the front in the same way.

tip Remember that chain at the beginning of a row counts as the first stitch. So the 2 chains skipped at the beginning of row 1 of the base of the bag comprise one stitch in the final count, as does the one chain made at the beginning of each following row.

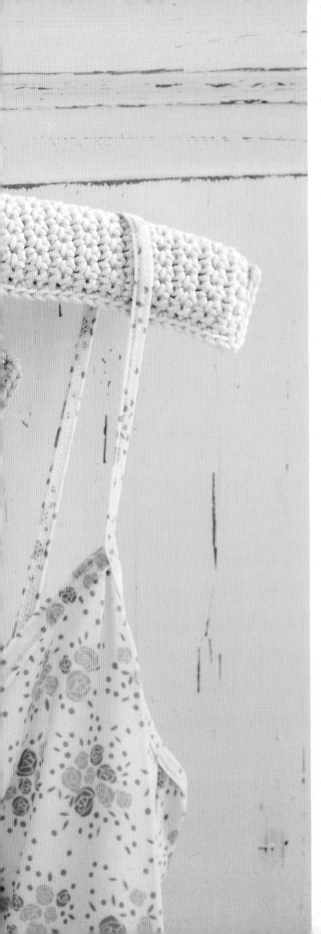

Clothes Hanger

Transform a plain wooden coat hanger into a luxury item with few crochet skills and even less sewing.

The cover of the hanger is a rectangle of single crochet, joined with single crochet on the right side for a neat, professional-looking finish.

You will need

1 x 100g ball of Sirdar Pure Cotton DK in pale green
3.50mm (Size E/4 U.S.) hook
Wooden coat hanger
Lightweight quilt batting
Scissors, sewing thread and needle
Ribbon
Tapestry needle

Gauge

8 stitches and 10 rows to 2in (5cm) over sc

Abbreviations

Ch – chain; cm – centimeters; in – inches;
sc – single crochet

COVERING THE HANGER

The cover

Cut out a rectangle of quilt batting to fit over and along the coat hanger.

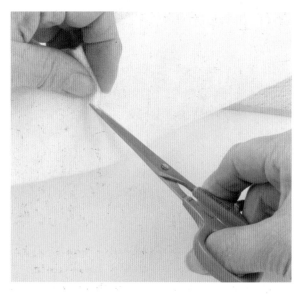

Fold the quilt batting in half lengthwise, snip a small hole in the center of the fold and push the hook of the hanger through.

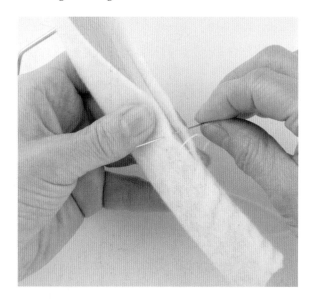

Join the cut edges of the quilt batting with whip stitch.

Chain 6 15 (or required odd number of ch to fit around padded hanger).

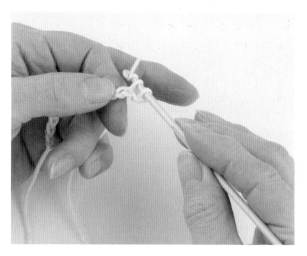

ROW 1 Skip 2 ch, *1 **single crochet 10** in next ch; repeat from * to end. 14 stitches (or an even number of stitches).

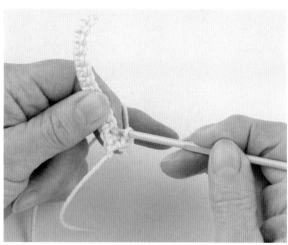

ROW 2 Ch 2, *1 sc in next sc; repeat from *, ending 1 sc in top ch of 2 ch.
Repeat row 2 until the crochet is the length of the padded hanger and an even number of rows has been completed.
Fasten off 21.

Finishing

Fold the crochet in half lengthwise and push the hook of the hanger through the center.
Join with single crochet 22. Starting at the fold, taking the hook under 2 strands of yarn each time,

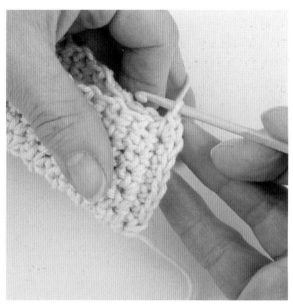

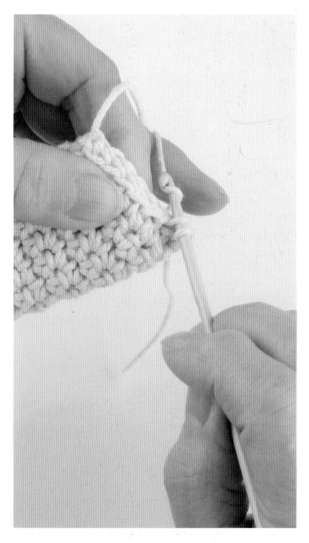

ends along the long edge, 3 sc in corner. Inserting the hook in the remaining single strand of each chain, complete second short edge to match the first.
Fasten off.
Trim with ribbon bow.

insert the hook in the first stitch of the front and corresponding stitch of the back, yarn over hook and pull through a loop, yarn over hook and pull through 2 loops to make a sc. Work a sc in each pair of stitches, 3 sc in corner, 1 sc in each pair of front and back row

Striped Cushion

Color is the key ingredient of this simple, stylish cushion with its cord-like edging.

The entire project, including the edging, is in single crochet. The last row of the edging is worked from left to right instead of right to left, which takes a little getting used to, but it isn't difficult.

Size
12in x 16in (30cm x 40cm)

You will need
9 x 50g balls Debbie Bliss Cotton Double Knitting:
    5 balls taupe (A)
    2 balls ivory (B)
    1 ball chocolate (C)
    1 ball turquoise (D)
4.00mm (Size G/6 U.S.) hook
4.50mm (Size 7 U.S.) hook
Pillow form

Tension
14 sts and 17 rows to 4in (10cm) over sc with larger hook

Abbreviations
Cm – centimeters; ch – chain; in – inches; sc – single crochet; sts – stitches

MAKING THE CUSHION

Back

With larger hook and A, **chain**  6 43.

ROW 1 Skip 2 ch, * 1 **single crochet** 10 in next ch; rep from * to end. 42 sts.

ROW 2 Ch 1, [1 sc in next sc] 40 times, 1 sc in top ch of 2 ch.

ROW 3 Ch 1, [1 sc in next sc] 40 times, 1 sc in ch.

Rep last row 19 times. Total 22 rows.

With B, work 14 rows.

With C, work 2 rows.

With D, work 8 rows.

With A, work 22 rows.

Fasten off 21.

Front

Work as for back, but do not fasten off.

Finishing

Matching stripes, place front on back, wrong sides together. With front facing, starting with a long side and using the smaller hook and A, **join with single crochet** 22: insert hook under 2 strands of first st of front and under 2 strands of corresponding st of back, yarn over hook and pull through a loop, yarn over hook again and pull it through 2 loops to make a sc.

Continue like this, working a sc in pairs of stitches and

working 3 sc in each corner, until 1 short side and 2 long sides have been joined.

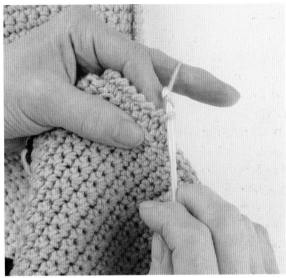

Along second short side work 1 sc in each st of front only to leave an opening for the pillow form, join with a slip stitch to the first sc. Do not fasten off. With front still facing, work sc from left to right (sometimes called crab or shrimp stitch).

Yarn over hook and pull it through 2 loops to complete sc. Work all stitches in this way. Fasten off.
Insert pillow form and stitch opening closed.

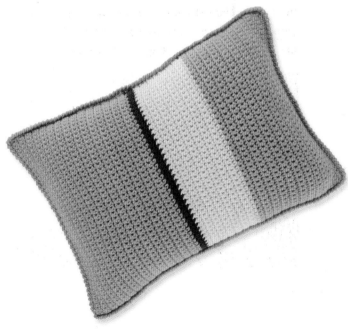

Insert hook under 2 strands of next sc on right, yarn over hook, pull through a loop to make 2 loops on the hook.

41

Belt

Crochet-covered rings can be made into a belt or even an entire garment if you feel experimental and want real 1960s' nostalgia.

For a beginner, working around a solid object like a curtain ring can be a way to keep the stitches even.

Size
33in (83cm) long, or required length, plus ties

You will need
3 x 50g balls Jaeger Aqua:
    1 ball pink (A)
    1 ball purple (B)
    1 ball orange (C)
2.75mm (Size C/2 U.S.) hook
22 curtain rings, approximately 1in (3cm) diameter
2 smaller rings
Tapestry needle

Gauge
Sc to fit fairly closely around ring

Abbreviations
Cm – centimeters; ch – chain; in – inches; sc – single crochet

MAKING THE BELT

To make

Using yarn color A,

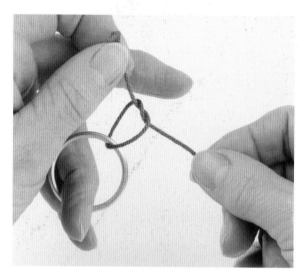

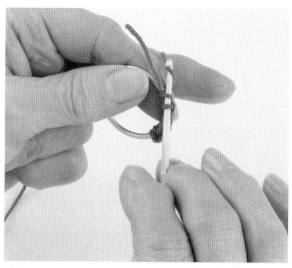

Repeat from * 31 times or until ring is filled with stitches.

make a single knot on one curtain ring (this replaces the usual slip knot).

Insert hook in ring, pull loop through,

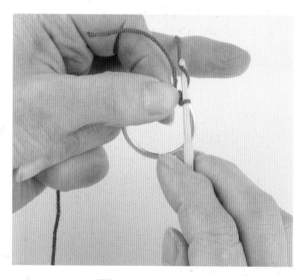

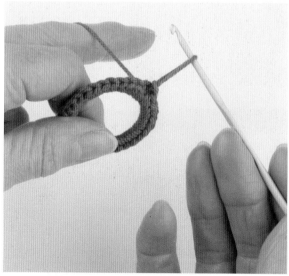

yarn over hook 4 and pull through loop on hook, *insert hook in ring, pull loop through, yarn over hook, pull through 2 loops (1 **single crochet** 10 made).

Fasten off 21, leaving an end to sew with. Thread this end on to a tapestry needle and join by taking it over the first sc of the round, under the two top strands of the next sc, then back into the last sc of the round, so that it looks like the top of a sc. **Darn in** 24 the first end, but leave the second free. Cover remaining large rings with B, C and A.

Tie

With C, cover 1 small ring with 20 sc or required number of stitches, **slip stitch** to first sc, **chain** 150, work 20 sc or required number around second small ring,

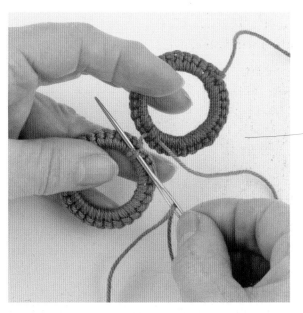

Finishing

Join two large rings by using the free end of one to stitch, on the wrong side, to a point opposite the free end of the second. Continue joining the rings in this way, then **darn in** the last end. Thread the tie through the end rings.

slip stitch to first sc.
Fasten off.

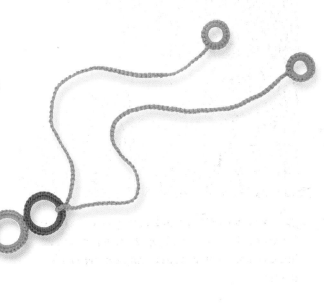

2

Double crochet

Double crochet is a taller stitch than single crochet, allowing more freedom to make open textures as well as fast-growing fabrics. You just have to remember to take the yarn over before inserting the hook, then everything follows logically. These projects are very varied but only hint at the possibilities that double crochet has to offer.

Striped Scarf

This long fringed scarf is made very special with the use of a sleek luxury yarn in wonderful rich colors.

The foundation chain is worked with a size larger hook to avoid puckering. Then each stripe is one row of double crochet and the fringe is attached with the crochet hook.

Size
3½in x 51in (9cm x 128cm) plus fringe

You will need
5 x 50g balls Debbie Bliss Cathay:
  2 balls purple (A)
  2 balls shocking pink (B)
  1 ball orange (C)
4.50mm (Size 7 U.S.) hook
5.00mm (Size H/8 U.S.) hook

Gauge
16 sts and 10 rows to 4in (10cm) over dc with the smaller hook

Abbreviations
Cm – centimeters; ch – chain; dc – double crochet; in – inches; rep – repeat; st(s) – stitch(es)

MAKING THE SCARF

With larger hook and A, **chain** **6** 206.
Change to smaller hook.

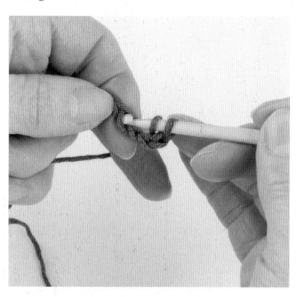

ROW 1 Skip 3 ch.
* 1 **double crochet** **11** in next ch;

repeat from * to end. 204 sts.

ROW 2 With B, ch 3,

* 1 dc in next dc.
Repeat from * to last st,

1 dc in top ch of 3 ch.

ROW 3 With A, ch 3, * 1 dc in next dc; repeat from * to last st, 1 dc in top ch of 3 ch.

ROW 4 Repeat row 2.

ROW 5 Repeat row 3.

ROW 6 Repeat row 2.

ROW 7 Repeat row 3.

ROW 8 Repeat row 2.

ROW 9 With C, repeat row 2.

Fasten off 21 .

Finishing

Lightly damp press.

Fringe the ends, matching each tassel to a stripe. A tassel consists of 5 strands of yarn, each strand approximately 12in (30cm) long.

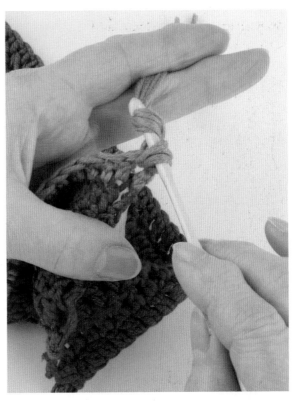

Hook the ends through the loop and pull up firmly. Comb the fringe to separate the individual strands within the yarn.

Double the 5 strands and then hook them through a row end to make a loop.

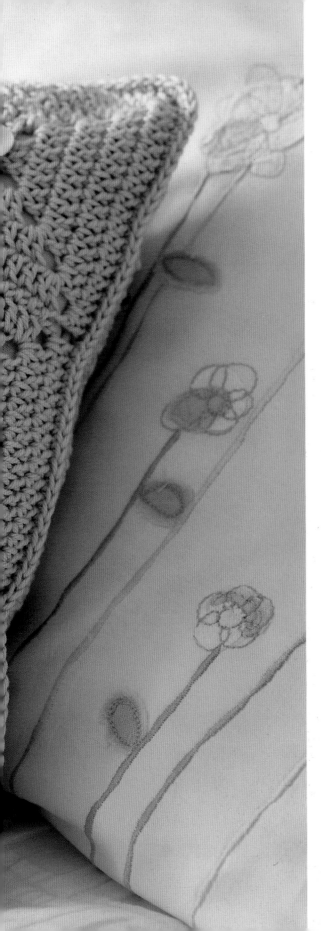

Cushion with Buttons

Achieve a quilted look by adding a mother-of-pearl button to the center of each square of a pastel-colored patchwork.

The first pieced project, this cushion is made up of squares made with chain and double crochet, then joined with single crochet on the wrong side.

Size
Approximately 11½in x 11½in (29cm x 29cm)

You will need
5 x 50g balls Jaeger Aqua in grey-blue
3.25mm (Size D/3 U.S.) hook
9 mother-of-pearl buttons
Pillow form

Gauge
Each square measures approximately 3½in (9cm)

Abbreviations
Cm – centimeters; ch – chain; ch sp – chain space;
dc – double crochet; in – inches; rep – repeat;
sc – single crochet; sl st – slip stitch; sp – space

MAKING THE CUSHION

Square

(make 18)

Chain 6 5, **slip stitch** 7 into first ch to form a **ring** 9.

Working in **rounds** 14 with right side facing:

ROUND 1 Ch 3, 2 **double crochet** 11 in ring, ch 3, * 3 dc in ring, ch 3;

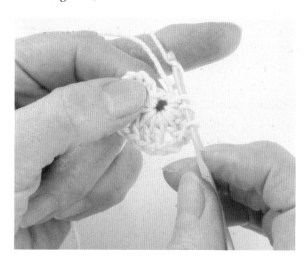

rep from * twice, sl st to top ch of 3 ch.

ROUND 2 Ch 3,

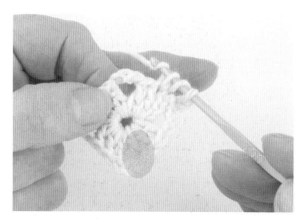

1 dc in each of next 2 dc, (2 dc, ch 3, 2 dc) in ch sp, * 1 dc in each of next 3 dc, (2 dc, ch 3, 2 dc) in ch sp; rep from * twice, sl st to top ch of 3 ch.

ROUND 3 Ch 3, 1 dc in each of next 4 dc, (2 dc, ch 3,

2 dc) in ch sp, * 1 dc in each of next 7 dc, (2 dc, ch 3, 2 dc) in ch sp; rep from * twice, 1 dc in each of next 2 dc, sl st to top ch of 3 ch.

ROUND 4 Ch 3, 1 dc in each of next 6 dc, (2 dc, ch 3, 2 dc) in ch sp, * 1 dc in each of next 11 dc, (2 dc, ch 3, 2 dc) in ch sp; rep from * twice, 1 dc in each of next 4 dc, sl st to top ch of 3 ch.

Fasten off 21.

Finishing

Set out two blocks of 9 squares each, the joins of each round facing in the same direction.

With right sides together, take 2 squares and **join with single crochet** 22: insert the hook under 2 strands of the first dc of 15 dc of front square and

under 2 strands of the corresponding dc of the back square, yarn over hook, and pull through a loop, yarn over hook again and pull it through 2 loops to make a sc.

Joining only the groups of 15 dc, join the remaining 7 squares of the back in the same way, then join the 9 squares of the front.

Edging
Back: with right side facing, **join the yarn** [20] at one corner and work

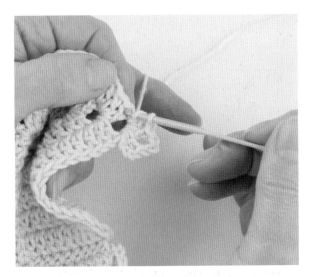

(ch 3, 1 dc, ch 3, 2 dc) in corner sp, * 1 dc in each of next 15 dc, [2 dc in last sp of this motif, ch 1, 2 dc in first sp of next motif, 1 dc in each of next 15 dc] twice, (2 dc, ch 3, 2 dc) in corner sp; rep from * along each side, joining last side to first with sl st in top ch of 3 ch.
Edge the front to match.
Fasten off.

Press to shape.
Join the back and front with sc: wrong sides together and working through 2 strands of each pair of stitches, work (ch 1, 2 sc) in one corner sp, * 1 sc in each of next 19 dc, 1 sc in 1-ch sp; rep from * once, 1 sc in each of next 19 dc, 3 sc in corner sp. Continue in this way along 2 more sides, working 3 sc in corners, to the last side and work into the front only along this side to leave an opening for the pillow form, sl st to 1 ch.
Fasten off.
Sew a button to the center of each square of the front. Insert the pillow form and stitch the opening closed.

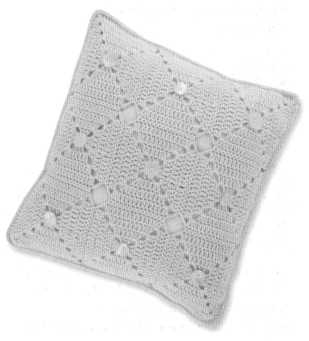

Baby's Garland

These friendly teddy bear faces and colorful pompons should enchant a very young baby.

Rounds of double crochet make all the crochet components of the teddies. Minimal sewing and embroidery skills are needed to complete the project.

Size

Approximately 11in (28cm) long, including pompons

You will need

3 x 50g balls Jaeger Matchmaker Double Knitting:
    1 ball camel (A)
    1 ball chocolate (B)
    1 ball turquoise (C)
3.25mm (Size D/3 U.S.) hook
Small quantity stuffing
Tapestry needle
Cardboard
Ribbon

Gauge

9 sts and 5 rows to 2in (5cm) over dc

Abbreviations

Cm – centimeters; ch – chain; dc – double crochet; in – inches; sl st – slip stitch; sts – stitches

MAKING THE GARLAND

Bear head

(make 2 pieces for each bear)

ROUND 1 With A, make a **slip ring 16**, **chain 6** 3, 11 **double crochet 11** in ring,

pull ring tight, sl st to top ch of 3 ch. 12 sts. **

ROUND 2 Ch 3, 1 dc in sl st of round 1, [2 dc in next dc] 11 times, sl st to top of 3 ch. 24 sts.

ROUND 3 Ch 3, 2 dc in next dc,

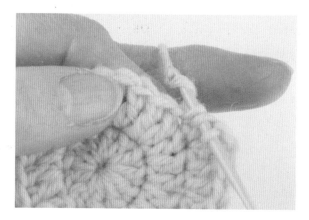

[1 dc in next dc, 2 dc in next dc] 11 times, sl st to top ch of 3 ch. 36 sts.

Fasten off 21.

Muzzle and ears

(make 3 pieces for each bear)

With A, work as head to **. Fasten off, leaving an end long enough to sew with.

Finishing

Push center of muzzle forward and coil first end inside to pad it. Place muzzle, its join downward, just below center of one head piece, also join downward.

Use second end to stab stitch it in place along inner edge of top 2 strands of each stitch.

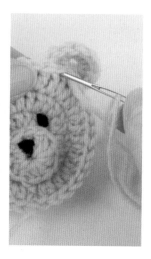

With B, embroider nose in satin stitch and eyes with French knots.

Stab stitch ears to face. Place face on back head piece and stab stitch the front and back together.

Push stuffing into the head before completing.

Pompoms

With C, make pompons: for each pompon, cut 2 discs of cardboard with a hole in the center.

Cut around the edge. Slip a length of yarn between the discs and tie, sliding out the discs and leaving ends long enough to sew with. Take the ends through each head just below the ears and secure with a few back stitches.

Attach ribbons at each end of the garland.

Wrap both with yarn until full.

Hippy Handbag

Sling it over your shoulder or use it as a
decorative hold-all around the home. Enjoy
the off-beat colors used here or design
your own palette.

These squares mix chain, single and
double crochet in a project that's entirely
crochet – no sewing is needed at all.

Size
Approximately 9in x 9in (23cm x 23cm)

You will need
7 x 50g balls Rowan Cotton Glace:
    1 ball green (A)
    1 ball turquoise (B)
    1 ball lilac (C)
    1 ball yellow (D
    1 ball blue (E)
    2 balls purple (F)
2.75mm (Size C/2 U.S.) hook

Gauge
One square measures 3in (7.5cm)

Abbreviations
Cm – centimeters; ch – chain; ch sp – chain space;
dc – double crochet; in – inches; sc – single crochet;
sl st – slip stitch; sp – space; st(s) – stitch(es)

MAKING THE HANDBAG

Square

(make 18)

With A, **chain**  6,

slip stitch  into first ch to form a **ring** . Work in **rounds**  with right side facing:

ROUND 1 Ch 3, work 15 **double crochet**  in ring, sl st to top ch of 3 ch.
16 sts.

ROUND 2 Ch 4, [1 dc in next dc, ch 1] 15 times,

sl st to 3rd of 4 ch.
Fasten off  A.

ROUND 3 **Join new yarn** . With B, pull loop through a ch sp,

then work (ch 3, 2 dc) in that sp, 3 dc in each of next 15 ch sp,
sl st to top ch of 3 ch.
Fasten off B.

ROUND 4 With C, pull loop through a sp between dc groups and ch 4, 1 **single crochet**  in next sp between dc groups [ch 3, 1 sc in next sp between dc groups] twice, *ch 5, 1 sc in next sp between dc groups [ch 3, 1 sc in next sp between dc groups] 3 times; rep from * twice more, ch 4,

sl st to first ch of 4 ch.

ROUND 5 Ch 1, 2 sc in first ch sp, 3 sc in each of next 2 ch sp, * (3 sc, ch 2, 3 sc) in corner sp,

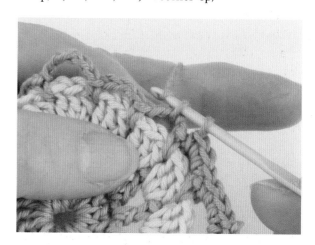

3 sc in each of next 3 ch sp; rep from * twice more, (3 sc, ch 2, 3 sc) in corner sp, sl st to 1 ch.
Fasten off C.
Make 17 more squares using the six colors in different combinations as shown.

Handles

(make 2)

With F, ch 150.

Skip 2 ch, 1 sc in each ch to end. Ch 2, without turning work over,

work 1 sc in each remaining strand of foundation ch. Fasten off.

Finishing

Press the squares to shape.

Assemble the squares in a rectangle, 3 across and 6 down.

With right sides together, **join 2 squares with single crochet 22**: with F, begin at corner 2-ch sp, insert hook under strands of first front edge stitch and strands of corresponding back edge stitch, yarn over hook and pull through a loop, yarn over hook again and pull it through 2 loops to make a sc.

Continue to join each pair of edge sts in this way, then, without fastening off, join the next pair of

squares in the same way. When all rows across have been completed, join the long rows to complete the rectangle.

Fold the rectangle, wrong sides together, and join side seams with single crochet: with F, working 1 sc in a pair of front and back sts each time.

Top edging

Working in rounds with right side facing:

ROUND 1 Starting at a side seam and using F, pull through a loop, ** ch 1, * 1 sc in next st;

repeat from * around front and back of bag, sl st to 1 ch.

ROUND 2 As round 1 from **.

Fasten off.

Sew on handles.

Slot-Through Scarf

If the motif looks familiar that's because the granny square, as it's sometimes called, is one of the most enduring crochet designs around.

Groups of double crochet and a few chains make up the square motifs. They're joined with single crochet and edged with picots – the decorative little blips which are simply 3 chains with a single crochet in the first chain.

Size
Approximately 5in (13cm) wide x 30in (78cm) long

You will need
6 x 50g balls Rowan 4 ply Soft:
    1 ball pink (A)
    1 ball lilac (B)
    1 ball lime (C
    1 ball turquoise (D)
    2 balls grey (E)
2.75mm (Size C/2 U.S.) hook

Gauge
One square measures approximately 2in (5cm)

Abbreviations
Cm – centimeters; ch – chain; ch sp – chain space; dc – double crochet; in – inches; rep – repeat; sc – single crochet; sl st – slip stitch; sp – space

MAKING THE SCARF

Square

(make 30)

With A, **chain** 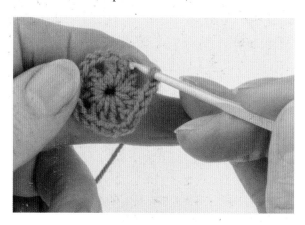 5, **slip stitch** 7 into first ch to form a **ring** 9 . Work in **rounds** 14 with right side facing:

ROUND 1 Ch 3, work 2 **double crochet** 11 in ring, ch 2, *3 dc, ch 2; rep from * twice,

sl st to top ch of 3 ch. **Fasten off** 21 .

ROUND 2 With B, **join yarn** 20 in first ch sp by pulling through a loop and then sl st, in same ch sp work (ch 3, 2 dc, ch 2, 3 dc), *in next ch sp work (3 dc, ch 2, 3 dc); rep from * twice,

sl st to top ch of 3 ch.
Fasten off.

ROUND 3 With E, join yarn in first ch sp of this round as before, in same ch sp (ch 3, 2 dc, ch 2, 3 dc), in sp between groups work 3 dc, * in next ch sp work (3 dc, ch 2, 3 dc), in sp between groups work 3 dc; rep from * twice, sl st to top ch of 3 ch.

Fasten off.

Make 29 more squares, repeating this color combination and substituting other colors for A and B, but always working round 3 with E.

Finishing

Press squares to shape.

Assemble scarf in 2 rows of 15 squares.

With right sides together and using E, take the first pair of squares and **join with single crochet** 22 : inserting the hook under the inner strand only of each pair of stitches, work 1 sc in corner ch,

1 sc in each of 9 dc, 1 sc in next corner ch.
Fasten off.

Join additional squares in the same way until there are
2 strips of 15 squares each. Join the long center seam in
the same way, leaving an opening between squares on
the fourth row from one end. With right side facing and
using E, work a row of sc along the 2 sides of this
opening.

Edging

Round 1 Working in rounds with right side facing:
With E, join yarn to the first corner ch of a square
roughly midway along a 15-row edge, ch 1, 1 sc in
each of 9 dc, * 1 sc in next corner ch, 1 dc in seam
between squares, 1 sc in next corner ch, 1 sc in each
of 9 dc; rep from * to corner of scarf,

(2 sc in first ch, 1 sc in 2nd ch), then continue in this
way around the sides and into corners of scarf,
ending sl st to first ch.
ROUND 2 Ch 1, 1 sc in next sc, * ch 3,

1 sc in first of 3 ch (picot made), 1 sc in each of next 3
sc; rep from * around scarf, ending ch 3, 1 sc in first
of 3 ch, join with sl st to first ch.
Fasten off.

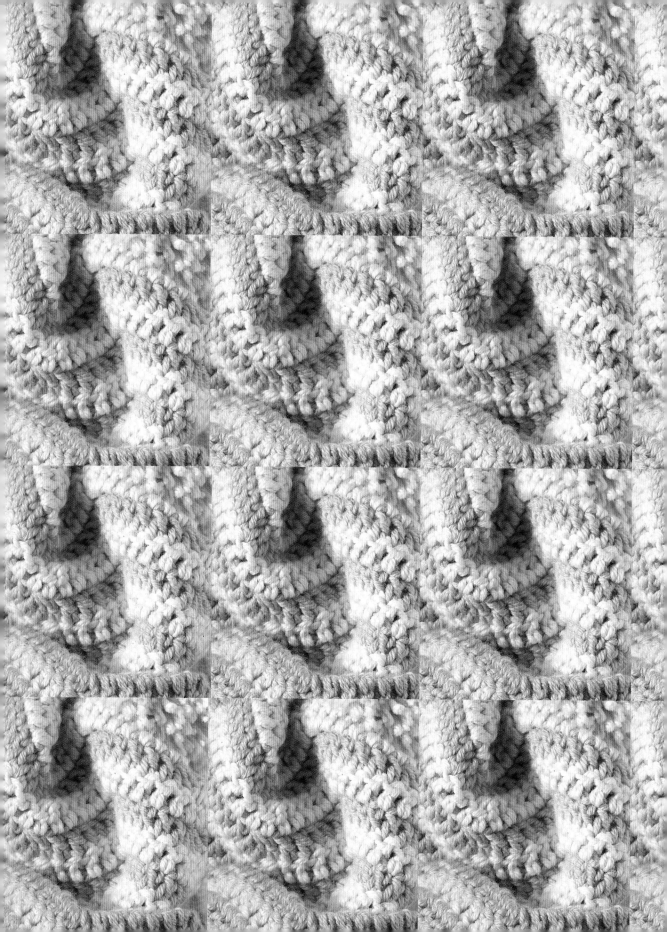

3

Shaping

Crochet is a wonderfully creative medium because there's no need for seams, no limit to the length of a row or a round and there's a multitude of effects you can achieve with increases and decreases.

If 'made' stitches (increases) are balanced by 'lost' stitches (decreases) the crochet is patterned but remains flat. Increases or decreases used alone will shape the fabric into curves, either at the edges or all over.

Hat with Brim

Wear this classic hat whichever way suits you best – with the brim turned back or right down over your eyes.

All the shapings are increases, which are very easy – they're simply two stitches instead of one. The rounds are continuous so it's best to use a marker of contrast yarn to keep count of stitches and rounds.

Size
To fit average adult

You will need
2 x 50g balls Jaeger Matchmaker Merino Aran
    in turquoise
5.50mm (Size I/9 U.S.) hook
6.00mm (Size J/10 U.S.) hook
Short length of contrast yarn for marker

Gauge
12 sts and 16 rows to 4in (10cm) over sc with the larger hook

Abbreviations
Cm – centimeters; ch – chain; in – inches;
sc – single crochet

MAKING THE HAT

ROUND 1 Make a **slip ring** .
With larger hook, **chain** 6 2, work 11 **single crochet** 10 in ring,

Insert **yarn marker** 15 before starting each round. The illustration shows the yarn marker lying between rounds.

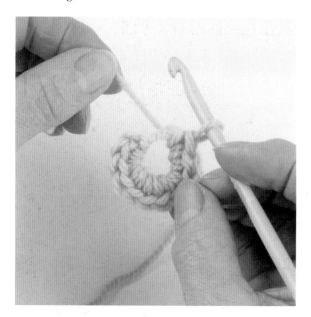

pull ring tight, **slip stitch** 7 to the top ch of 2 ch. 12 sts. Keeping the right side facing, work in **rounds** 14.

The illustration shows an increase being made by working 2 sc into 1 sc.

ROUND 2 1 sc in top ch of 2 ch, 2 sc in first sc of round 1, [1 sc in next sc, 2 sc in next sc] 5 times. 18 sc.

ROUND 3 [1 sc in next sc, 2 sc in next sc] 9 times. 27 sc.

ROUND 4 1 sc in each sc.

ROUND 5 [1 sc in each of next 2 sc, 2 sc in next sc] 9 times. 36 dc.

ROUNDS 6 AND 7 Repeat round 4.

ROUND 8 [1 sc in each of next 2 sc, 2 sc in next sc] 12 times. 48 sc.

ROUNDS 9, 10 AND 11 Repeat round 4.

ROUND 12 [1 sc in each of next 2 sc, 2 sc in next sc] 16 times. 64 sc.

ROUNDS 13 TO 24 Repeat round 4.

ROUND 25 [1 sc in each of next 3 sc, 2 sc in next sc] 16 times. 80 sc.

ROUNDS 26 TO 29 Repeat round 4.

ROUND 30 [1 sc in each of next 7 sc, 2 sc in next sc] 10 times. 90 sc.

ROUNDS 31 TO 33 Repeat round 4.

ROUND 34 With smaller hook, work 1 sc around each sc (that is, work into the round below instead of the top of the stitch).

Fasten off 21 .

Pull out marker, **darn in ends 24 .**

Pet Ball

Make a small, soft ball in single crochet as
an indoor toy for a pampered pet.

Rounds of increases are matched by
rounds of decreases to create a sphere. If
it isn't perfectly round this can be corrected
with firm stuffing!

Size

Circumference approximately 8½in (21cm)

You will need

1 x 50g ball Debbie Bliss Merino DK in lime
4.00mm (Size G/6 U.S.) hook
Stuffing
Short length of contrast yarn for marker
Tapestry needle

Gauge

9 sts and 10 rows to 2in (5cm) over sc

Abbreviations

Cm – centimeters; ch – chain; dec in next 2 sc –
decrease one st: [insert hook in next sc, yarn over
hook and pull loop through] twice, yarn round hook
and pull it through all 3 loops; in – inches; sc – single
crochet; sts – stitches

MAKING THE BALL

Working in **rounds** with right side facing:
ROUND 1 Make a **slip ring** , **chain** 2, work 11 **single crochet** in ring, pull ring tight,

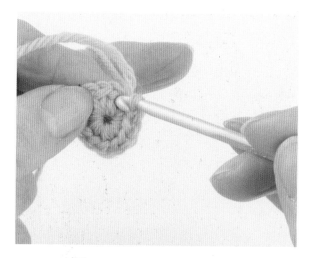

slip stitch to top ch of 2 ch. 12 sts.

Insert **yarn marker** before starting next and every round.

ROUND 2 1 sc in top ch of 2 ch, 2 sc in first sc, [1 sc in next sc,

2 sc in next sc] 5 times. 18 sc.

ROUND 3 [1 sc in each of next 2 sc, 2 sc in next sc] 6 times. 24 sc.

ROUND 4 1 sc in each of 24 sc.

ROUND 5 [1 sc in each of next 3 sc, 2 sc in next sc] 6 times. 30 sc.

ROUNDS 6 AND 7 1 sc in each of 30 sc.

ROUND 8 [1 sc in each of next 4 sc, 2 sc in next sc] 6 times. 36 sc.

ROUNDS 9, 10, 11 AND 12 1 sc in each of 36 sc.

ROUND 13 [1 sc in each of next 4 sc, 1 **decrease** in next 2 sc] 6 times. 30 sc.

ROUNDS 14 AND 15 Repeat round 6.

ROUND 16 [1 sc in each of next 3 sc, 1 dec in next 2 sc] 6 times. 24 sc.

ROUND 17 Repeat round 4.

ROUND 18 [1 sc in each of next 2 sc, 1 dec in next 2 sc] 6 times. 18 sc.

ROUND 19 [1 sc in next sc, 1 dec in next 2 sc] 6 times. 12 sc.

Finishing

Pull out marker and complete filling.

Thread end of yarn on to tapestry needle and use to gather up last 6 sts and then

whip stitch to match the other side of the ball.

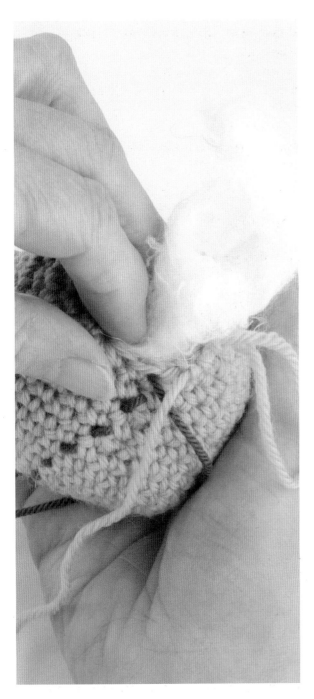

Push in most of stuffing, firmly and evenly.

ROUND 20 [1 dec in next 2 sc] 6 times. 6 sc.

Fasten off 21.

Rose

Instead of a brooch, pin a bold crochet rose to your jacket or jumper.

The flower is made in one strip. A row of double crochet has double and treble crochet scallops worked along it and is then gathered up. The stem is chain with slip stitch.

Size
Approximately 3in (7.5cm) across

You will need
1 x 50g ball of Jaeger Extra Fine Merino DK in pink
4.00mm (Size G/6 U.S.) hook
Tapestry needle

Gauge
9 sts to 2in (5cm) over dc

Abbreviations
Ch – chain; cm – centimeters; dc – double crochet; in – inches; sl st – slip stitch; tr – treble crochet: yarn over hook twice, insert hook into next stitch, yarn over hook, pull through a loop to make 4 loops on hook [yarn over hook, pull it through next 2 loops] 3 times; sts – stitches

MAKING THE ROSE

Leaving a fairly long end, **chain** **6** 71.

ROW 1 Skip 3 ch, 1 **double crochet** **11** in each ch to end. 69 sts.

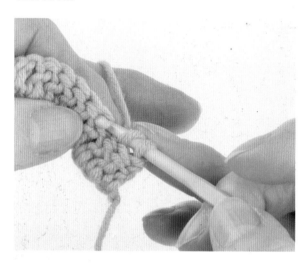

ROW 2 [Skip next 2 dc. 7 dc in next dc, skip next 2 dc,

7 **treble** (see abbreviations on page 79) in next dc. skip next 3 dc,

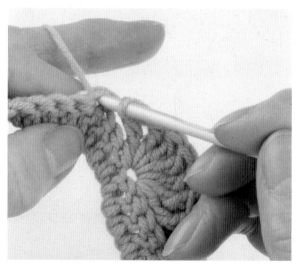

slip stitch **7** in next dc] 5 times. [Skip next 3 dc,

sl st in next dc] 4 times, skip next 3 dc, 7 tr in next dc, skip next 2 dc, sl st in top ch of 3 ch. 5 small petals and 5 larger petals made.

Fasten off **21**, leaving an end of wool long enough to sew with.

Finishing

Rose

Thread first end on to a tapestry needle and

run it under and over remaining strands of base chain.

Pull up to gather.

Starting with smaller petals, coil the strip, tightly at first and then more loosely, the spaces between petals alternating as far as possible. Stitch base of petals, using longer end of yarn.

Stem

Chain 16, skip 1 ch,

sl st in each ch to end.

Fasten off **21,** leaving an end long enough to sew the stem on with.

Zigzag Hat

Stripes are more interesting when they run in chevrons around a baby's hat.

Increases and decreases along the row cause the stripes to zigzag and the edge to wave. But these are all the shapings involved in this pattern, there's no shaping in the crown of the hat – the chevrons are pleated at the top.

Size
To fit a child age 6–12 months

You will need
2 x 50g balls of Rowan Wool Cotton:
    1 ball turquoise (A)
    1 ball lime (B)
3.50mm (Size E/4 U.S.) hook
4.50mm (Size 7 U.S.) hook
Tapestry needle

Gauge
14 sts (one repeat) and 7 rows to 3in (7cm) over dc with smaller hook

Abbreviations
Ch – chain; cm – centimeters; dc – double crochet; double dec – double decrease: [yarn over hook, insert hook in next dc, yarn over hook and pull loop through, yarn over hook and pull it through 2 loops on hook] 3 times, yarn over hook and pull it through all 4 loops on hook; in – inches; st(s) – stitch(es).

MAKING THE HAT

With larger hook and A, **chain 6** 73.
Change to smaller hook.

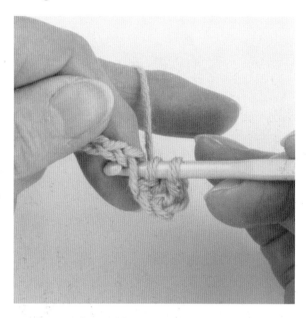

ROW 1 Skip 3 ch, 2 **double crochet 11** in next ch,
1 dc in each of next 4 ch,

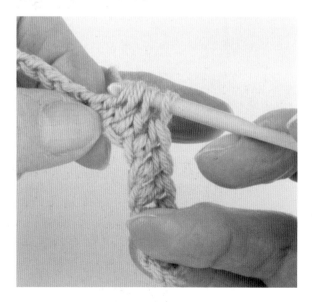

[**double decrease** (see abbreviations on page 82) in
next 3 ch, 1 dc in each of next 5 ch,

3 dc in next ch, 1 dc in each of next 5 ch] 4 times,
double dec in next 3 ch, 1 dc in each of next 5 ch,

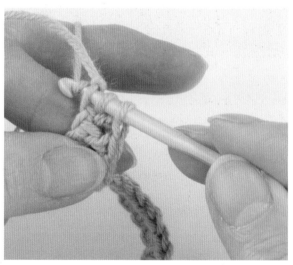

2 dc in last ch. 71 sts.

ROW 2 With B, ch 3, 1 dc in st below, 1 dc in each of
next 5 sts, [double dec in next 3 sts, 1 dc in each of
next 5 sts, 3 dc in next st, 1 dc in each of next 5 sts]
4 times, double dec in next 3 sts, 1 dc in each of next
5 sts, 2 dc in top ch of 3 ch.

ROW 3 With A, repeat row 2.

Repeat rows 2 and 3

9 times.

Fasten off 21.

Finishing

On the wrong side at the top, pinch the V-shaped chevrons to form folds. Stitch each pair of edges, taking in both strands of each stitch. When all five chevrons are joined, sew about half of the back seam on the wrong side from the top, then reverse the seam for the turn-back cuff.

Make a pompon (see page 59) with B and attach to the top of the hat.

Baby Brogues

These quirky little booties would make a perfect present for a young baby.

There's quite a lot of shaping involved in making the curves, but the project is tiny and there's almost no sewing required.

Size
To fit 0–3 months

You will need
1 50g ball of Jaeger Matchmaker Merino Aran
    in dusky pink
4.50mm (Size 7 U.S.) hook
Short length of contrast yarn for marker
Tapestry needle
Ribbon

Gauge
7 sts and 9 rows to 2in (5cm) over sc

Abbreviations
Cm – centimeters; ch – chain; ch sp – chain space; dec in next 2 dc – decrease one st: [insert hook in next sc, yarn over hook and pull loop through] twice, yarn over hook and pull it through all 3 loops on hook; in – inches; sc – single crochet; sl st – slip stitch; sp – space; st(s) – stitch(es)

MAKING THE SHOES

Main part

(starting with the sole)

Chain 6 8.

Work in **rounds** 14 with right side facing:

ROUND 1 Skip 3 ch,

1 **single crochet** 10 in each of 5 ch, ch 2, without turning work over, 1 sc in each remaining single strand of 5 ch, 1 sc in next ch, 2 ch, **slip stitch** 7 to next ch. Insert **yarn marker** 15 before starting next and following rounds.

ROUND 2 1 sc in next ch, 1 sc in each of next 5 sc, 3 sc in 2-ch sp, 1 sc in each of next 6 sc, 3 sc in 2-ch sp. 18 sc.

ROUND 3 [1 sc in each of next 6 sc, 2 sc in each of next 3 sc] twice. 24 sc.

ROUND 4 [1 sc in each of next 6 sc,

2 sc in each of next 6 sc] twice. 36 sc.

ROUNDS 5 AND 6 1 sc in each sc.

ROUND 7 [1 sc in each of next 2 sc, dec in next 2 sc, 1 sc in each of next 2 sc] 6 times. 30 sc. Work 1 sc in each of next 3 sc beyond marker.

Turn and now work in **rows** 12 for back extension:

ROW 1 (wrong side) Ch 1, 1 sc in sc below, 1 sc in each of next 10 sc, 2 sc in next sc, turn. 14 sts.

ROWS 2 TO 8 Ch 1, 1 sc in each of next 12 sc, 1 sc in ch. **Fasten off** 21, leaving an end of yarn long enough to sew with.

Top

(worked in rounds like the sole)

Ch 5.

ROUND 1 Skip 3 ch, 1 sc in each of 2 ch, ch 2, without turning work over, 1 sc in each remaining single strand of 2 base ch, 1 sc in next ch, ch 2, **slip stitch** 7 in next ch of 3 ch. Insert yarn marker before starting next and following rounds.

ROUND 2 1 sc in next ch, 1 sc in each of next 2 sc, 3 sc in 2-ch sp, 1 sc in each of next 3 sc, 3 sc in 2-ch sp. 12 sts.

ROUND 3 [1 sc in each of next 3 sc, 2 sc in each of next 3 sc] twice. 18 sc.

ROUND 4 1 sc in each of next 3 sc, 2 sc in each of next 6 sc] twice. 30 sc. Work 1 sc in each of next 2 sc beyond marker. Do not fasten off.

Finishing

Take top and main part and **join with single crochet 22:** wrong sides together, place top on main part of shoe and, starting beside back extension and using attached yarn,

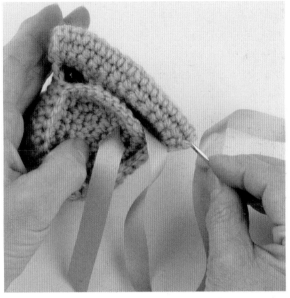

insert hook under both strands of next sc of top and next sc of main part, yarn over hook, pull loop through, yarn over hook and pull it through both loops on hook to complete a sc. Continue in this way until 18 pairs of stitches have been joined. Fasten off.

Thread ribbon through the casing and bring the ends out through the stitches of the top front.
Tie in a bow and trim the ends.

Fold back extension in half to the right side and stitch it down along the edge to make a casing.

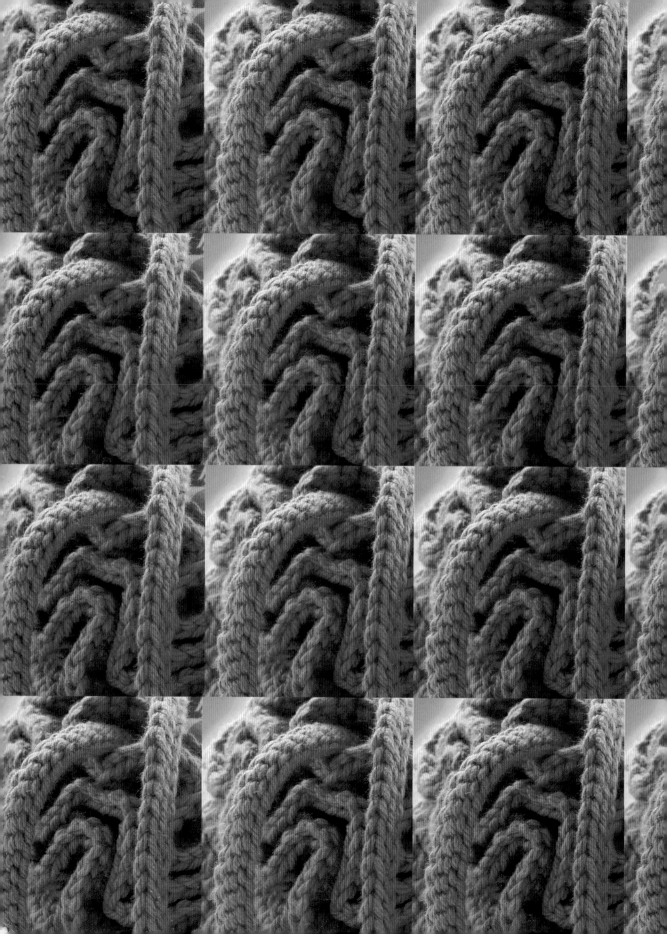

4 Special Techniques

Still using simple stitches, but in new combinations, these designs explore some new directions in crochet. Some are larger-scale projects than before, others introduce treble crochet which, as its name suggests, is taller even than double crochet. They all require a little confidence and good basic skills.

String Bag

Sturdy denim yarn makes this a user-friendly update on the old-fashioned string bag.

The main part is an easy mesh pattern of chain, single and double crochet, starting from a circular base and finishing with single crochet.

Size
Approximately 10in (25cm) wide and 11in (28cm) long

You will need
2 x 50g balls Rowan Denim in pale blue
3.50mm (Size E/4 U.S.) hook

Gauge
Based on a tension of 4 mesh to 4in (10cm)

Abbreviations
Ch – chain; cm – centimeters; ch sp – chain space;
dc – double crochet; in – inches; rep – repeat;
sc – single crochet; sl st – slip stitch;
sts – stitches

MAKING THE BAG

Chain 6, **slip stitch** in first ch to join into a **ring** .

ROUND 1 Ch 4, [1 **double crochet** in ring, ch 1]

11 times, sl st in 3rd of 4 ch, sl st in next ch sp. You now have 12 ch sp.

ROUND 2 [ch 2, 1 **single crochet** in next ch sp] 11 times, ch 1, 1 sc in first of 2 ch.

ROUND 3 [ch 3, 1 sc in next ch sp] 11 times, ch 2, 1 sc in first of 3 ch.

ROUND 4 [ch 4, 1 sc in next ch sp] 11 times, ch 3, 1 sc in first of 4 ch.

ROUND 5 [ch 5, 1 sc in next ch sp] 11 times, ch 2, 1 dc in first of 5 ch.

ROUND 6 [ch 6, 1 sc in next ch sp] 11 times, ch 3, 1 dc in first of 6 ch.

ROUND 7 [ch 6, (1 sc, ch 6, 1 sc) in next ch sp, ch 6, 1 sc in next ch sp] 5 times, ch 6, (1 sc, ch 6, 1 sc) in next ch sp, ch 3,

1 dc in first of 6 ch.

18 ch sp.

ROUND 8 [ch 6, 1 sc in next ch sp] 17 times, ch 3, 1 dc in first of 6 ch.

ROUND 9 [ch 6, (1 sc, ch 6, 1 sc) in next ch sp, (ch 6, 1 sc) in each of next 2 ch sp] 5 times, ch 6, (1 sc, ch 6, 1 sc) in next ch sp, ch 6, 1 sc in next ch sp, ch 3, 1 dc in first of 6 ch. 24 ch sp.

ROUND 10 [ch 6, 1 sc in next ch sp] 23 times, ch 3, 1 dc in first of 6 ch.

Repeat last round 18 times.

ROUND 29 [ch 3, 1 sc in next ch sp] 23 times, ch 3, sl st in first of 3 ch].

Finishing

Edging

ROUND 30 Ch 1,

[3 sc in 3-ch sp, 1 sc in sc] 23 times, 3 sc in 3-ch sp, sl st in 1 ch. 96 sts.

ROUND 31 Ch 1, 1 sc in each sc, ending sl st in 1 ch. Do not break yarn.

Handles

First handle ** Ch 52, turn, skip 1 ch,

1 sc in each ch, sl st into nearest sc of edging, ch 2, turn so that 2 ch lie to inside of bag, sl st into sc of edging nearest other side of handle, half turn, along second side of handle.

work 1 sc in remaining strand of each sc.

Fasten off 21, leaving end long enough to stitch this part of handle to bag.

Second handle: On opposite side of bag, right side facing, sl st into 1 sc of edging, work as first handle from **.

Without twisting them, sew ends of handles to edging.

Ribbed Cushion

Strongly-defined ribs give this simple cushion its firm fabric and bold texture.

The ribs are made by working treble crochet over and around stitches. This is one of those techniques that is much easier than it looks and the patterning is only done on the right side.

Size

Approximately 14in x 14in (35cm x 35cm)

You will need

10 x 50g balls Debbie Bliss Cotton DK
4.00mm (Size G/6 U.S.) hook
Pillow form

Gauge

16 sts and 13 rows to 4in (10cm) over pattern

Abbreviations

Cm – centimeters; ch – chain; dc – double crochet;
sc – single crochet; sl st – slip stitch; sts – stitches;
tr b – treble crochet made around a stitch 2 rows
below: yarn over hook twice, skip sc row below, insert
hook under next stitch of row below from right to
left, bringing hook out on right side, yarn over hook,
pull through loop (4 loops on hook), [yarn over hook,
pull it through 2 loops] 3 times

MAKING THE CUSHION

Back

Chain 6 57.

ROW 1 (right side) Skip 3 ch,

[1 **double crochet 11** in next ch] 54 times. 55 sts.

ROW 2 Ch 1,

[1 **single crochet 10** in next dc] 53 times, 1 sc in top ch of 3 ch.

ROW 3 Ch 3, 1 dc in next sc,

1 **treble below** (see abbreviations on page 97) around 3rd st of first row, [1 dc in next sc, 1 tr b in next but one dc of first row] 25 times, 1 dc in next sc, 1 dc in 1 ch.

ROW 4 Ch 1, [1 sc in next st] 53 times, 1 sc in top ch of 3 ch.

ROW 5 Ch 3, 1 dc in next sc,

1 tr b around first tr b, [1 dc in next to last sc of last row, 1 tr b around next tr b] 25 times, 1 dc in next to last sc of last row, 1 dc in ch.

ROWS 4 AND 5 form pattern.

Repeat rows 4 and 5 another 21 times, thus ending with a right side row.

Do not fasten off.

Edging

ROUND 1 With right side facing, (ch 1, 2 sc) in first corner, working under two strands of yarn each time work 1 sc in each sc and 2 sc in each dc of first side, 3 sc in corner, 1 sc in each remaining strand of base ch, 3 sc in corner, work third side same as first side,

Finishing

Place back and front with wrong sides together, **join with single crochet 22:** ch 1, insert hook under both strands of first st of front and both strands of first st of back, make a sc in the usual way, continue to make 1 sc in each pair of sts and 3 sc in the center sc at each corner to the last side.

Insert the pillow form and complete round 2 with sl st to 1 ch.

Fasten off 21.

3 sc in corner, 1 sc in each st of fourth side, sl st to 1 ch.

Front

Work as back.

Clothes Cover

Open effects can appear rather daunting to a beginner, but this chunky edging is quite simple and could be put to all kinds of uses around the home.

It's worked repeat-by-repeat lengthwise so you simply stop when you have the length you require. The ring that starts the repeat is joined with a treble crochet but that's the only unusual feature of the stitch pattern.

You will need

1 x 100g ball of Sirdar Pure Cotton DK in white
3.50mm (Size E/4 U.S.) hook
Cotton or linen fabric, paper, sewing thread
Wooden coat hanger

Gauge

1 pattern measures approximately 1½ in (4cm) long

Abbreviations

Cm – centimeters; ch – chain; in – inches; sc – single crochet; tr – treble: yarn over hook twice, insert hook, yarn over hook, pull through loop (4 loops on hook), [yarn over hook, pull it through 2 loops] 3 times

MAKING THE COVER

Lace

To make the lace edging, ** **Chain** **6** 8.

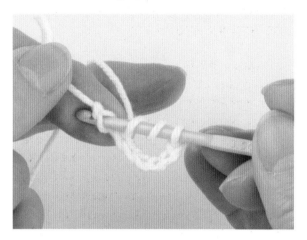

1 **treble** (see abbreviations on page 100) in first ch, turn.

ROW 1 Ch 1,

6 **single crochet** **10** around half of 8 ch, turn.

ROW 2 Ch 1, 1 sc in each of next 5 sc, 1 sc in ch, turn.

ROW 3 Ch 1, 1 sc in each of next 5 sc,

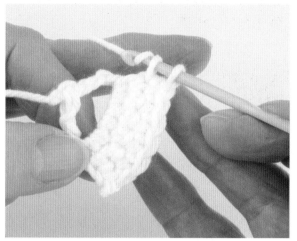

2 sc in ch, turn.

ROW 4 Ch 1, 1 sc in each of next 6 sc, 1 sc in ch, do not turn.

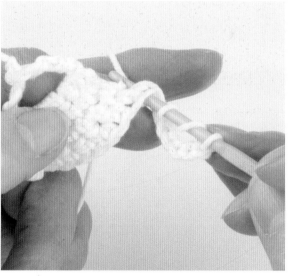

Repeat from ** until 20 patterns have been completed, or until lace is required length (check width of coat hanger and add a little to accommodate garment).

Do not fasten off.

Edging

When working in row ends insert hook under two strands of yarn as usual: Ch 1,

1 sc in each of next 3 sc row ends, * 4 sc around tr, 1 sc in each of next 4 sc row ends; repeat from *, ending 3 sc around tr, 1 sc in first ch.
Fasten off 21.

Finishing

Pin out lace to required length, keeping top edge straight and pinning the points to shape. Press, using steam or a damp cloth.

Make a paper pattern for the cover – the lower edge to fit the lace doubled, the top shaped by drawing around the coat hanger and adding a ¾in (2cm) seam allowance around all edges. Cut out 2 fabric pieces. Right sides together, stitch these around sides and top, leaving an opening for the hook. Neaten this opening and seams. Turn through to right side. Make a small hem along lower edge and hand stitch the lace to this, joining the ends neatly at one side seam. Spray starch, if required.

Bath Mat

Treat your toes to a firm white cotton bath mat with a textured star design.

The bobbles forming the star are called popcorns. Because a popcorn is a group of double crochets gathered with a single stitch at the top it's both very well defined and durable.

Size

Approximately 16½ in x 24½ in (41cm x 61cm)

You will need

3 x 100g balls Sirdar Pure Cotton DK
3.50mm (Size E/4 U.S.) hook

Gauge

18 dc and 10 rows to 4in (10cm) over dc

Abbreviations

Cm – centimeters; ch – chain; dc – double crochet; in – inches; pc – popcorn: work 5 dc in next st, take out hook leaving loop, insert hook from front to back in top of first dc then into loop, yarn over hook, pull yarn through both loop and dc; rep – repeat; st(s) – stitch(es)

MAKING THE MAT

Mat

Chain **6** 77.

ROW 1 Skip 3 ch, * 1 **double crochet** **11** in next ch; repeat from * to end. 75 sts.

ROW 2 Ch 3, * 1 dc in next dc; repeat from *, ending 1 dc in top ch of 3 ch.

Repeat row 2 sixteen times, making a total of 18 rows.

Making a popcorn

To make a popcorn (pc),

Take out the hook, leave the loop and insert the hook from front to back in the first dc of the group of 5.

first make 5 dc in the next stitch.

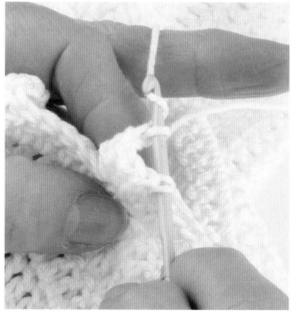

Insert the hook in the loop, yarn over hook and pull it through both loop and dc to complete the popcorn.

ROW 19 (right side) Ch 3, [1 dc in next dc] 36 times, 1 popcorn in next dc, [1 dc in next dc] 36 times, 1 dc in top ch of 3 ch.

ROW 20 (On wrong-side rows a double crochet and a popcorn are both now referred to as a st) Ch 3, * 1 dc in next st; repeat from *, ending 1 dc in top ch of 3 ch.

ROW 21 Ch 3, [1 dc in next dc] 34 times, 1 pc in next dc, 1 dc in each of next 3 dc,

1 pc in next dc, [1 dc in next dc] 34 times, 1 dc in top ch of 3 ch.

ROW 22 and wrong-side rows Repeat row 20.

ROW 23 Ch 3, [1 dc in next dc] 32 times, [1 pc in next dc, 1 dc in each of next 3 dc] twice, 1 pc in next dc, [1 dc in next dc] 32 times, 1 dc in top ch of 3 ch.

ROW 25 Ch 3, [1 dc in next dc] 18 times, [1 pc in next dc, 1 dc in each of next 3 dc] 9 times, 1 pc in next dc, [1 dc in next dc] 18 times, 1 dc in top ch of 3 ch.

ROW 27 Ch 3, [1 dc in next dc] 20 times, [1 pc in next dc, 1 dc in each of next 3 dc] 8 times, 1 pc in next dc, [1 dc in next dc] 20 times, 1 dc in top ch of 3 ch.

ROW 29 Ch 3, [1 dc in next dc] 22 times, [1 pc in next dc, 1 dc in each of next 3 dc] 7 times, 1 pc in next dc, [1 dc in next dc] 22 times, 1 dc in top ch of 3 ch.

ROW 31 Ch 3, [1 dc in next dc] 24 times, [1 pc in next dc, 1 dc in each of next 3 dc] 6 times, 1 pc in next dc, [1 dc in next dc] 24 times, 1 dc in top ch of 3 ch.

ROW 33 Repeat row 29.

ROW 35 Repeat row 27.

ROW 37 Repeat row 25.

ROW 39 Repeat row 23.

ROW 41 Repeat row 21.

ROW 43 Repeat row 19.

Now work 18 repeats of row 20.

Total 61 rows.

Fasten off 21 .

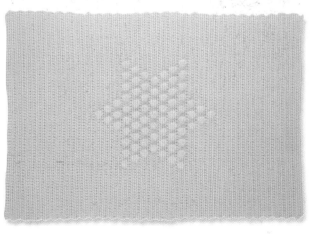

Baby Blanket

Wrap baby in a generous warm blanket that's chequered in two toning colors.

Patterning two colors together instead of separately is tricky at first, but with a little patience it becomes routine to change color in mid stitch and to carry one yarn invisibly by working around it with the other.

Size

Approximately 30½ in x 41in (77cm x 102cm)

You will need

11 x 50g balls of Jaeger Baby Merino DK:
    5 balls lilac (A)
    6 balls pale lilac (B)
5.00mm (Size H/8 U.S.) hook
4.50mm (Size G/6 U.S) hook

Gauge

17 sts and 9 rows to 4in (10cm) over pattern with smaller hook

Abbreviations

Cm – centimeters; ch – chain; cc – color change: with first color, yarn over hook, insert hook in next st, yarn over hook and pull through to make 3 loops on hook, yarn over hook and pull it through the next 2 loops on hook, change to 2nd color, yarn over hook, pull yarn through 2 remaining loops to complete dc; dc – double crochet; in – inches; rep – repeat; sl st – slip stitch; st(s) – stitch(es)

MAKING THE BLANKET

Changing color

Changing a color halfway through making a stitch (abbreviation cc) gives a neater result than changing between stitches.

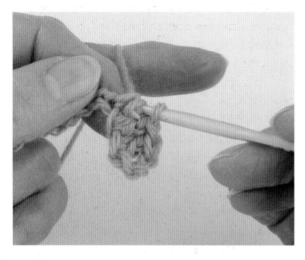

With color A, yarn over hook, insert hook in next st, yarn over hook and pull through to make 3 loops on hook, yarn over hook and pull through the next 2 loops on the hook.

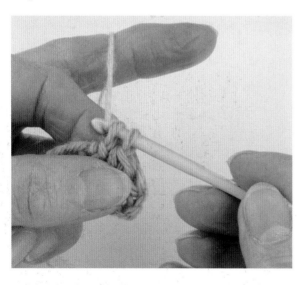

With second color, yarn over hook, pull yarn through 2 remaining loops to complete a dc.

Blanket

With larger hook and A, **chain** **6** 121.
Change to smaller hook.
ROW 1 (right side) Skip 3 ch, 1 **double crochet** **11** in each of next 2 ch, **change color** (see instructions, left) in next ch, * with B,

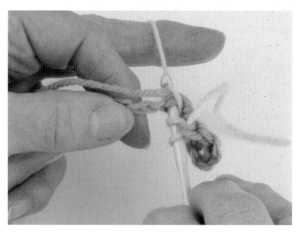

working each dc around A, 1 dc in each of next 2 ch, cc in next ch, with A, working each dc around B, 1 dc in each of next 2 ch, cc in next ch; rep from *, ending with A, but not working around B,

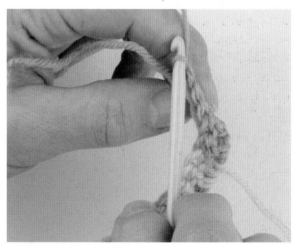

1 dc in each of next 4 ch.
119 sts.

ROW 2 With A, ch 3, 1 dc in each of next 2 dc, cc in next dc, * working around color not in use as before, with B, 1 dc in each of next 2 dc, cc in next dc, with A, 1 dc in each of next 2 dc, cc in next dc; rep from *,

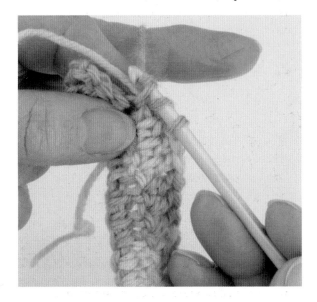

ending with A, working around B, 1 dc in each of next 3 dc, 1 dc in top ch of 3 ch. Continue to work around color not in use when it needs to be carried to a new block of color.

ROW 3 With B, ch 3, 1 dc in each of next 2 dc, cc in next dc, * with A, 1 dc in each of next 2 dc, cc in next dc, with B, 1 dc in each of next 2 dc, cc in next dc; rep from *, ending with B, 1 dc in each of next 3 dc, 1 dc in top ch of 3 ch.

ROW 4 Repeat row 3.

ROW 5 With A, ch 3, 1 dc in each of next 2 dc, cc in next dc, * with B, 1 dc in each of next 2 dc, cc in next dc, with A, 1 dc in each of next 2 dc, cc in next dc; rep from *, ending with A, 1 dc in each of next 3 dc, 1 dc in top ch of 3 ch.

Rep rows 2–5 twenty times, then work row 2 again. 86 rows.

Fasten off 21.

Edging

With right side facing, using smaller hook and B:

ROUND 1 **Join yarn 20** in top right hand corner, (ch 3, 2 dc) in corner st, * 1 dc in each st to next corner, 3 dc in corner, 2 dc around each dc to next corner, * 3 dc in corner; rep from * to *, ending at first corner, **slip stitch 7** to top ch of 3 ch.

ROUND 2 Ch 3, 3 dc in next st, * 1 dc in each st to next corner, 3 dc in 2nd of 3 dc; rep from *, ending sl st to top ch of 3 ch.

ROUND 3 Ch 3, 1 dc in next st, 3 dc in next st, * 1 dc in each st to next corner, 3 dc in 2nd of 3 dc; rep from *, ending sl st to top ch of 3 ch.

ROUND 4 With A and starting in one corner, (ch 1, 1 **single crochet 10**) in corner st, * 1 sc in each st to next corner, 2 sc in corner st; rep from *, ending sl st to 1 ch.

Fasten off. **Darn in ends 24.**

Press.

Ruffled Scarf

Although it may look like a boa, this long scarf is designed to be worn coiled round the neck in flattering ruffles.

It grows quickly because the stitch is treble crochet with some chain. Lots of increases make the crochet curl and spiral.

Size
Approximately 50in (125cm) long

You will need
2 x 50g balls Debbie Bliss Cotton Cashmere in crimson
5.50mm (Size I/9 U.S.) hook

Gauge
5 sts and 2 rows to 2in (5cm) over tr

Abbreviations
Cm – centimeters; ch – chain; in – inches; rep – repeat; sc – single crochet; tr – treble: yarn over hook twice, insert hook, yarn over hook, pull through a loop to make 4 loops on hook, [yarn over hook, pull it through next 2 loops on hook] 3 times;

MAKING THE SCARF

Scarf

Chain **6** 160.

ROW 1 Skip 3 ch, * 1 **treble** (see abbreviations on page 113) in next ch;

ROW 2 Ch 4,

1 tr in tr below, * 2 tr in next tr; repeat from *, ending 2 tr in top ch of 3 ch.

ROW 3 Ch 5,

repeat from *, ending 2 tr in last ch.

* 1 tr in next tr, ch 1; repeat from *, ending 1 tr in top ch of 4 ch.

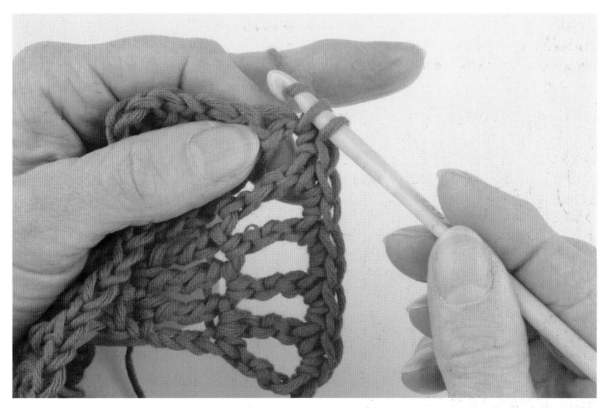

ROW 4 Ch 1, * 2 **single crochet** 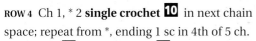 in next chain space; repeat from *, ending 1 sc in 4th of 5 ch. **Fasten off** 21 . **Darn in ends** 24 .

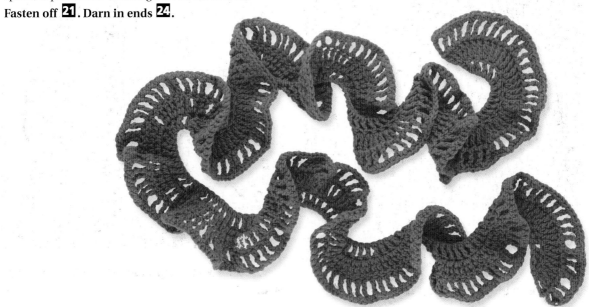

Frilly Bag

An explosion of frills around the top is the main feature of this frivolous little handbag.

The frills are a good example of an interesting effect achieved with simple stitches. Three rounds of open mesh around the top of the bag (double crochet and chain) are used as a base for closely-worked double crochets, which then stand away from the bag as crisp frills.

Size
Approximately 7½in wide x 6in high (19cm x 16cm)

You will need
3 x 50g balls of Rowan Handknit Cotton
3.25mm (Size D/3 U.S.) hook
3.50mm (Size E/4 U.S.) hook

Gauge
18 dc and 10 rows to 4in (10cm) with larger hook

Abbreviations
Cm – centimeters; ch – chain; dc – double crochet; in – inches; sc – single crochet; sl st – slip stitch; sp – space(s); sts – stitches

MAKING THE BAG

Sides

With larger hook, **chain** 6 72 and without twisting, join with **slip stitch** 7 to form a ring 9.

Work in **rounds** 14 with right side facing:

ROUND 1 Ch 3, 1 **double crochet** 11 in each ch to end, without twisting sl st to top ch of 3 ch. 72 sts.

ROUND 2 Ch 3, 1 dc in each dc to end, sl st to top ch of 3 ch. Repeat round 2 nine times.

ROUND 12 Ch 5,

[skip 2 dc, 1 dc in next dc, ch 2] 22 times, sl st to 3rd of 5 ch. 24 sp.

ROUND 13 Ch 5, [1 dc in next dc, ch 2] 22 times, sl st to 3rd of 5 ch.

ROUND 14 Repeat round 13.

Fasten off 21.

Frill

With smaller hook:

ROUND 1 Folding back rounds 12–14 to be out of the way, **join yarn** 20 to first dc of round 11, ch 3, 1 dc in this dc and

2 dc in next dc, * turn work 45 degrees, fold along

first dc of round 12 and work 4 dc around the post of this dc, * turn, fold and work 4 dc around 2 ch, turn, fold and work

4 dc around post of next dc, turn, fold and work

2 dc in each of next 2 dc of round 11, turn, fold and work

4 dc around post of next dc; repeat from *, ending 4 dc around 2 ch, 4 dc around first 3 ch of 5 ch, sl st to top ch of 3 ch.

Fasten off.

ROUND 2 In first sp of round 12 join yarn and ch 3, 3 dc around 2 ch, turn and fold, 4 dc around post of first dc of round 13, * turn and fold, 4 dc around 2 ch, turn and fold, 4 dc around post of next dc, turn and fold, 4 dc around 2 ch, turn and fold, 4 dc around post of next dc; repeat from *, ending 4 dc in 2 ch, 4 dc in first 3 ch of 5 ch, sl st to top ch of 3 ch. Fasten off.

ROUND 3 Starting in first sp of round 13, work as round 2. Fasten off.

ROUND 4 In first sp of round 14 join yarn and ch 1, 2 **single crochet** 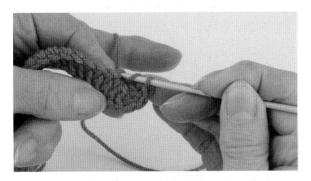 **10** around 2 ch, * ch 3, 3 sc around next 2 ch; repeat from *, ending 3 ch, sl st to 1 ch. Fasten off.

Base

With larger hook, ch 30.
ROUND 1 Skip 3 ch, 1 dc in each of next 26 ch,

5 dc in last ch, without turning work over, work 1 dc in each remaining single strand of 26 ch, 4 dc in first of 3 ch, sl st to top ch of 3 ch. 62 sts.
ROUND 2 Ch 3, 1 dc in each of next 26 dc, 2 dc in each of next 5 dc, 1 dc in each of next 26 dc, 2 dc in each of next 4 dc, 1 dc in sl st, sl st to top ch of 3 ch. 72 sts. Fasten off.

Handles

(make 2)
With larger hook, ch 100.
Skip 1 ch, * sl st in next ch; repeat from * to end, 1 ch, sl st in the remaining single strand of each of 99 ch. Fasten off, leaving an end long enough to sew with.

Finishing

Flatten sides so that join forms side seam, then match side seam to center 10 dc of base. Place base and sides wrong sides together and using smaller hook, **join with single crochet 22,** inserting hook in a single strand of a base ch of sides and an edge stitch of base each time.

On each side, pull a handle through an open space in last row of frills, join the ends and secure the join to the bag.

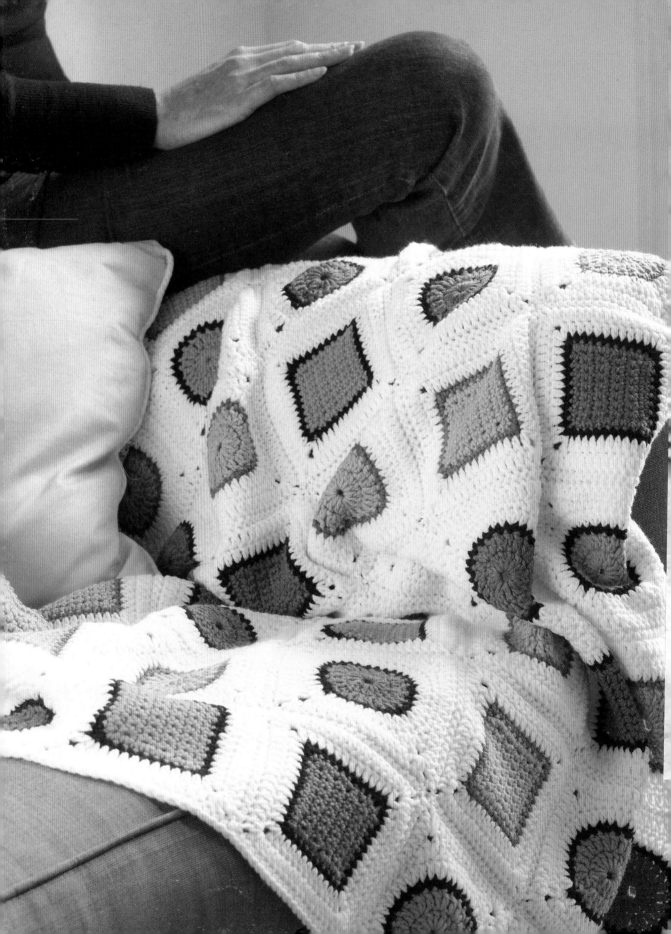

Retro Throw

There's something deliberately reminiscent of the 1960s in this geometric and almost monochromatic woolen throw.

The circular motif is constructed in rounds and then its corners are squared up. The center of the square motif is worked in rows for a well-defined shape and then it is completed in rounds so that all the edges match.

Size

Approximately 29in x 44in (73cm x 109cm)

You will need

15 x 50g balls of Jaeger Extra Fine Merino DK
    2 balls charcoal (A or B)
    2 balls flannel (A)
    1 ball black (B)
    1 ball lime (A)
    9 balls white (C)
4.50mm (Size 7 U.S.) hook

Gauge

Each square measures approximately 5in (13cm)

Abbreviations

Cm – centimeters; ch – chain; ch sp – chain space; dc – double crochet; in – inches; sc – single crochet ss – slip stitch; st(s) – stitch(es)

MAKING THE THROW

Square motif

(make 25)

With A, **chain** 6 10.

ROW 1 Skip 2 ch, 1 **single crochet** 10 in each of next 8 ch. 9 sts.

ROW 2 Ch 1, 1 sc in each of next 7 sc, 1 sc in top ch of 2 ch.

ROW 3 Ch 1, 1 sc in each of next 7 sc, 1 sc in ch.

Repeat row 3 six times, making a total of 9 rows. Do not fasten off and do not turn work over.

Now work in **rounds** 14 with right side facing:

ROUND 1 Around the square work: ch 3, 1 sc in each of 8 row ends, (1 sc, 2 ch, 1 sc) in last row end, 1 sc over each of 7 sts of 1st row, (1 sc, 1 ch, 1 sc) in last st of row, 1 sc in each of 7 row ends, (1 sc, ch 1, 1 sc) in last row end,

1 sc in each of 7 sts of last row, join with **slip stitch** 7 to first of 3 ch.

Fasten off 21 A.

ROUND 2 With B, pull through a loop in one corner ch sp to **join yarn** 20, ch 3, 1 sc in ch sp, [1 sc in each of next 9 sc,

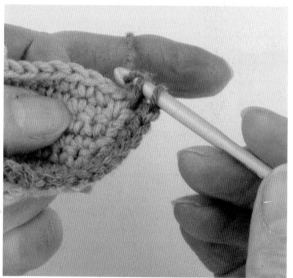

(1 sc, ch 2, 1 sc) in corner ch sp] 3 times, 1 sc in each of next 8 sc, 1 sc in sl st, sl st to first of 3 ch. 44 sts plus corner ch.

Fasten off B.

ROUND 3 With C, pull through a loop in one corner ch sp, ch 5, 1 **double crochet** 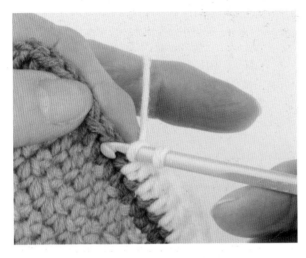 in ch sp, [1 dc in each of next 11 sc, (1 dc, ch 2, 1 dc) in corner ch sp] 3 times,

1 dc in each of next 10 sc, 1 sc in sl st, sl st to 3rd of 5 ch, sl st in 5-ch sp. 52 sts plus corner ch.

ROUND 4 Ch 3, (1 dc, ch 2, 2 dc) in 5-ch sp,

[1 dc in each of next 13 dc, (2 dc, ch 2, 2 dc) in corner ch sp] 3 times, 1 dc in each of next 12 dc, 1 dc in sl st, sl st to top ch of 3 ch. 68 sts plus corner ch.
Fasten off.

Round motif

(make 29)

With A, ch 5, sl st into first ch to make a **chain ring** .

ROUND 1 Ch 3, 15 dc in ring, sl st to top ch of 3 ch. 16 sts.

ROUND 2 Ch 3, [2 dc in next dc, 1 dc in next dc] 7 times, 2 dc in next dc, sl st to top ch of 3 ch. 24 sts. Fasten off A.

ROUND 3 With B, pull through a loop in next st to join yarn, ch 1, [2 sc in next dc,

1 sc in next dc] 11 times, 2 sc in next dc, sl st to 1 ch. 36 sts.
Fasten off B.

ROUND 4 With C, pull through a loop in next st, ch 3, 1 dc in next sc, [2 dc in next sc, 1 dc in each of next 2 sc] 11 times, 2 dc in next sc,

sl st to top ch of 3 ch. 48 sts.

ROUND 5 Ch 5, 1 dc in base of 1st ch, 1 dc in next dc, [1 sc in each of next 9 dc, 1 dc in next dc, (1 dc, ch 2, 1 dc) in next dc, 1 dc in next dc] 3 times,

1 sc in each of next 9 dc, 1 dc in next dc, sl st to 3rd of 5 ch, sl st in 5-ch sp. 52 sts plus corner ch.

ROUND 6 Ch 3, (1 dc, ch 2, 2 dc) in 5-ch sp, [1 dc in each of next 13 sts, (2 dc, ch 2, 2 dc) in corner ch sp] 3 times,

1 dc in each of next 12 sts, 1 dc in first sl st of previous round, sl st to top ch of 3 ch. 68 sts plus corner ch.
Fasten off.

Make a total of 54 motifs: 8 square motifs with charcoal as A and black as B, 10 with flannel as A and charcoal as B, 7 with lime as A and black as B; 10 round motifs with charcoal as A and black as B, 11 with flannel as A and charcoal as B, 8 with lime as A and black as B. All squares have white as C.

Finishing

Damp press the squares to shape. Arrange the squares in a rectangle of 6 across and 9 down, with all final ends lying in the same direction. With right sides together and using C, take pairs of squares and **join with single crochet 22 ,** inserting the hook under inner strand of each edge stitch until all the shorter rows have been joined, then join all the longer rows.

Edging

With right side facing and using C, starting with 1 ch in any square, * work 1 sc in each edge st,

1 dc in each seam and 3 sc in each corner, ending sl st in 1 ch.
Fasten off.

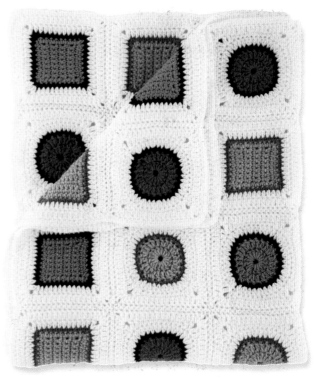

Yarn Information

The following information will help you to make a substitution if the yarn used in a project is not available. Be sure to check the pattern, look at the ball bands, and compare the new yarn with the information below to be sure the substitution is an appropriate one. Remember that the people who work in the store should be both knowledgeable and eager to help.

Debbie Bliss Cathay
Double-knitting-weight cotton, viscose, and silk yarn
50% Cotton/35% Viscose/15% Silk
Approximately 108yds (100m) per
1¾oz (50g) ball

Debbie Bliss Cotton Cashmere
Double-knitting-weight cotton and cashmere
85% cotton/15% cashmere
Approximately 103yds (95m) per
1¾oz (50g) ball

Debbie Bliss Cotton DK
Double-knitting-weight cotton
100% cotton
Approximately 91yds (84m) per
1¾oz (50g) ball

Debbie Bliss Merino DK
Double-knitting-weight wool
100% merino wool
Approximately 120yds (110m) per
1¾oz (50g) ball

Jaeger Aqua
Double-knitting-weight cotton
100% mercerized cotton
Approximately 116yds (106m) per
1¾oz (50g) ball

Jaeger Baby Merino DK
Double-knitting-weight wool
100% merino wool
Approximately 130yds (120m) per
1¾oz (50g) ball

Jaeger Extra Fine Merino DK
Double-knitting-weight wool
100% extra-fine merino wool
Approximately 137yds (125m) per
1¾oz (50g) ball

Jaeger Matchmaker DK
Double-knitting-weight wool
100% merino wool
Approximately 130yds (120m) per
1¾oz (50g) ball

Jaeger Matchmaker Merino Aran
Aran-weight merino wool
100% merino wool
Approximately 90yds (82m) per
1¾oz (50g) ball

Rowan 4-ply Soft
4-ply wool yarn
100% merino wool
Approximately 190yds (175m) per
1¾oz (50g) ball

Rowan Cotton Glace
Lightweight cotton yarn
100% cotton
Approximately 125yds (115m) per
1¾oz (50g) ball

Rowan Denim
Medium-weight cotton yarn
100% cotton
Approximately 101yds (93m) per
1¾oz (50g) ball

Rowan Handknit Cotton
Medium-weight cotton yarn
100% cotton
Approximately 92yds (85m) per
1¾oz (50g) ball

Rowan Wool Cotton
Double-knitting-weight wool and cotton
50% merino wool/50% cotton
Approximately 123yds (113m) per
1¾oz (50g) ball

Sirdar Pure Cotton DK
Double-knitting-weight cotton
100% cotton
Approximately 184yds (169m) per
3½oz (100g) ball

Yarn Suppliers

ROWAN & JAEGER YARNS

USA
Westminster Fibers Inc.
4 Townsend West
Suite 8
Nashua, NH 03063
Tel: +1 603 886 5041
Email:
rowan@westminsterfibers.com

Canada
Diamond Yarn
9697 St Laurent
Suite 101
Montreal
Quebec H3L 2N1
Tel: +1 514 388 6188
E-mail:
diamond@diamondyarn.com
www.diamondyarn.com

Australia
Australian Country Spinners
314 Albert Street
Brunswick
VIC 3056
Tel: +61 (0)3 9380 3888

UK
Rowan
Green Lane Mill
Holmfirth
West Yorkshire HD9 2DX
Tel: +44 (0)1484 681881
www.knitrowan.com

DEBBIE BLISS YARNS

USA
Knitting Fever Inc.
315 Bayview Avenue
Amityville, NY 11702
Tel: +1 516 546 3600
Email: admin@knittingfever.com
www.knittingfever.com

Canada
Diamond Yarn
155 Martin Ross Avenue
Unit 3
Toronto
Ontario M3J 2L9
Tel: +1 416 736 6111
E-mail:
diamond@diamondyarn.com
www.diamondyarn.com

Australia
Sunspun
185 Canterbury Road
Canterbury
VIC 3126
Tel: +61 (0)3 9830 1609
Email: shop@sunspun.com.au

Jo Sharp Pty Ltd
PO Box 1018
Freemantle
WA 6959
Tel: +61 (0)8 9430 9699
Email: yarn@josharp.com.au

UK
Designer Yarns Ltd
Units 8-10 Newbridge Industrial
Estate
Pitt Street
Keighley
West Yorkshire BD21 4PQ
Tel: +44 (0)1535 664222
www.designeryarns.uk.com

SIRDAR YARNS

USA
Knitting Fever Inc.
315 Bayview Avenue
Amityville, NY 11702
Tel: +1 516 546 3600
Email: admin@knittingfever.com
www.knittingfever.com

Canada
Diamond Yarn
9697 St Laurent
Suite 101
Montreal
Quebec H3L 2N1
Tel: + 1 514 388 6188
Email:
diamond@diamondyarn.com
www.diamondyarn.com

Diamond Yarn
155 Martin Ross Avenue
Unit 3
Toronto
Ontario M3J 2L9
Tel: + 1 416 736 6111
Email:
diamond@diamondyarn.com
www.diamondyarn.com

Australia
Creative Images
PO Box 106
Hastings
VIC 3915
Tel: + 61 (0)3 5979 1555
Email:
creative@peninsula.starway.net.au

UK
Sirdar Spinning Ltd
Flanshaw Lane
Alverthorpe
Wakefield
West Yorkshire WF2 9ND

Knitting and Crochet Titles

CROCHET

Classic Crocheted Vests

Crochet from the Heart NEW!

Crochet for Babies and Toddlers

Crochet for Tots

Crocheted Aran Sweaters

Crocheted Lace

Crocheted Socks!

Crocheted Sweaters

First Crochet NEW!

Fun and Funky Crochet NEW!

The Little Box of Crocheted
Hats and Scarves

**More Crocheted
Aran Sweaters NEW!**

Today's Crochet

KNITTING

200 Knitted Blocks

365 Knitting Stitches a Year:
Perpetual Calendar

Basically Brilliant Knits

Beyond Wool

Big Knitting NEW!

Classic Knitted Vests

Comforts of Home

Dazzling Knits

Fair Isle Sweaters Simplified

First Knits

Garden Stroll, A

Handknit Style

Knit It Now!

Knits for Children
and Their Teddies

Knits from the Heart

Knitted Shawls,
Stoles, and Scarves

Knitted Throws and More for
the Simply Beautiful Home

The Knitter's Book of
Finishing Techniques

A Knitter's Template

Knitting with Hand-Dyed Yarns

Knitting with Novelty Yarns

Lavish Lace

**The Little Box of Knitted
Ponchos and Wraps NEW!**

**The Little Box of
Knitted Throws NEW!**

The Little Box of Scarves

The Little Box of Scarves II

The Little Box of Sweaters

More Paintbox Knits

Perfectly Brilliant Knits NEW!

The Pleasures of Knitting

Pursenalities

Rainbow Knits for Kids

Sarah Dallas Knitting

Saturday Sweaters NEW!

Sensational Knitted Socks NEW!

Simply Beautiful Sweaters

Simply Beautiful Sweaters
for Men

Style at Large

A Treasury of Rowan Knits

The Ultimate Knitted Tee

The Ultimate Knitter's Guide

Martingale ®
& C O M P A N Y

America's Best-Loved Craft & Hobby Books®

America's Best-Loved Knitting Books®

Our books are available at bookstores and your favorite craft, fabric, and yarn retailers. If you don't see the title you're looking for, visit us at www.martingale-pub.com or contact us at:

1-800-426-3126

International: 1-425-483-3313

Fax: 1-425-486-7596

Email: info@martingale-pub.com

Acknowledgements

Thanks to Hilary Underwood, who
helped with the crochet, and to Susan
Horan, who checked the instructions.